PRISONERS OF EARTH

Psychic Possession and Its Release

by
Aloa Starr

Light Technology Publishing
P.O. Box 1526
Sedona, AZ
86339

2nd Edition Revised 1993
by Light Technology Publishing
ISBN 0-929385-37-3

Cover Painting by Carol Putnam Nye

Printed by Mission Possible Commercial Printing
A division of Love Light Communication Services
P.O. Box 1526, Sedona, AZ 86339

(Names and initials have been changed to protect the privacy of the persons involved)

CONTENTS

FOREWORD

When I received the invitation to write a foreword to Aloa Starr's book I felt honored and worried at the same time — honored because I value Aloa's friendship greatly and because I admire her dedication to the Healing Ministry of Release, and worried because I'm not a writer and I'm not sure I can live up to the task. One thing is sure: If I were a writer that's the book I would want to write.

In recent years the media has spread an array of sensational and fantastic information on the various phenomena of possession — information which has often no connection with the facts as they are. There are many degrees of possession and some of these are relatively common, more common than one would ever believe. So it is very important that the public become aware of the whole issue and that it learn to protect itself. Psychiatry and psychology have proposed models to explain these phenomena rationally while remaining within the limits of the premises established by these sciences. The phenomena, however, seem to surpass those limits. But this is not the right place for theoretical dissertations even if it would be a fascinating study in certain aspects.

In my opinion the special value of this book lies in the fact that it unmystifies the phenomenon of possession by revealing the numerous forms under which it manifests itself and by offering to the "patients" hope and a total and rapid liberation.

Dr. Louis Rodriguez, in his book "God Bless the Devil", recommends that psychiatrists of the future dedicate themselves to heal the disincarnate entities since he estimates that all mental illnesses are the outcome of psychic parasitism. He is not the only one to hold this view, although many of his colleagues prefer not to admit it publicly.

Certainly Aloa is not alone in engaging in this type of work and the positive results she obtains in this country are paralleled in many other countries. In Brazil, for instance, there is a hospital by the name of *Hospital Espirita* which has cured hundreds and hundreds of mental patients by means of techniques similar to those used by Aloa. The hospital keeps detailed and objective documentation of every single case treated.

But one more surprise awaits the reader of this book: Aloa herself. To perform successfully a work of this kind one has to lead a life pure in deed and intents, harbour a profound love for humanity, be moved by great dedication, and possess the necessary knowledge and authority. Without these qualities, the process of "Liberation" can put the operator in serious danger. Aloa Starr is one of these rare people.

Giovanni Boni, Ph.D., M.S., D.C.

PREFACE

"How did you get into this work of releasing discarnate entities?" people have asked me. The answer goes back to January of 1972 when I found that I had entities attached to my aura! A friend had asked me to accompany her to Phoenix to visit mutual friends who had just become involved in exorcising discarnate entities and demons from those who had requested this service. Ellen and I spent a fascinating weekend with this dedicated elderly couple. They told us how they had learned, during the past summer, to take measurements with a pendulum over a person's picture, handwriting, or in person to determine if there were any discarnate entity attachments on his aura. They had found that a person's vibrations flow through the fingers, pen, and ink and finally into the handwriting and can be picked up with a pendulum. But a photocopy or other facsimile will not work. Later we were sometimes sent a photocopy of a signature and it would be dead – no vibes at all. But interestingly, even a picture in a newspaper carries the personal vibrations.

They had by now worked up a release ritual and with the help of their spiritual guides and angelic helpers were having great success. Ellen asked them to check us out which they did. Ellen was clear, but to my surprise there were nine entities attached outside my aura, and they had all come in at the same time about eight years previously. Later I remembered a very traumatic event that had taken place. A release was done for me and that night I slept better than I had in years, and during the days that followed I discovered that the horrid little voice that used to torment me was GONE! Often just as I awoke in the morning, a voice in my head would say something stupid or obscene. "Who said that?" I would demand. "I wouldn't say that! You get out of here." I had prayed and worked on this often but it still persisted. Now it was gone!

All I could think of was that this was the work I wanted to do more than anything else.After consulting with their Teachers, the friends agreed to teach both Ellen and me as a team. However, Ellen soon dropped out because of continued psychic attacks and she felt this was not her work.

As the training progressed, I began to realize the scope of preparation I had already been given. For eight years, I had worked with a Light Group in California where healing and releases were done in class. This is where I became acquainted with Lone Wolf and Mighty Waterfall and their hundreds of Indian Runners who would answer our calls and lead away the discarnate entities. Then there were the In-God-We-Trust angels, who were seen as little cherubs, but powerful, carrying golden nets in which they placed the stubborn entities that refused to leave. Also, I had attended some meetings where a trance channel brought through the voices of discarnate entities (unattached) that wished to be released and we all helped to free them and send them on. The channel had a Chinese invisible master who came through first and kept the channel protected. Then too, I had been working with a pendulum for several years after reading Max Freedom Long's books.

Later, as my own work began, I incorporated the Indian runners and methods we had used over the years with the new techniques. We began with three or four requests and these grew, by word of mouth only, until thousands of people have been helped.

Sometimes I am asked if I "feel" or "see" anything when the discarnates are taken away. So far I am not clairvoyant, but I do feel a shudder up my back when they leave. However, all of them do not always leave at once, so it is my spiritual teachers who confirm to me, through the pendulum, that they have all been taken away. However, other clairvoyants have observed the discarnate entities being led away as well as the Indian Runners and In-God-We-Trust angels.

There has been so little written on the subject of exorcism that it seems appropriate at this time to share my experiences in this field. It was obvious, at the outset, that almost every one who wrote us had some kind of discarnate attachment and that I could not release the whole world! So I prayed, asking God to send only those who would truly benefit from the work, His children who were trying to serve Him but were being hindered from fulfilling their divine plan by these negative attachments which are also freed and led away to the planes where they belong. In the case of negative thoughtforms, which we term "demons", these are dissolved and transmuted by the Angels of the Violet Flame. We do not wish to unduly frighten our readers who may not be familiar with this type of attachment. But if it is present, and it is often the answer when nothing else has helped, it is better to find out and have it removed than to "hide under the covers" in fear. However, we feel that after reading this book and how the work is done, our readers will have more understanding and no fear.

Joyfully and gratefully I share this work with you.

Aloa Starr

v

Chapter 1

What Is Possession?

A few years ago a famous movie star was convicted of murdering his wife. In his testimony he maintained that he had absolutely no recollection of doing it – his mind had seemingly blanked it out. This has happened in many similar cases where the criminal, after coming to himself, is shocked and grief- stricken to find out what he has done. There are many cases of this nature on record for which science has no valid explanation.

Our understanding is that most of these people are possessed by negative discarnate entities who have taken over the body, temporarily blocking the person's own mind and memory. In the early days of our training, we practiced by making evaluations on photos from newspapers. In every case of a criminal act, the person was found to be possessed or partially possessed. We have found that there are degrees of entity attachment which will be explained later.

It is the understanding of many people that after a person makes the transition through death, there is always someone who comes to meet the deceased. This is only true for those who are computed to the higher planes. We are finding out now that after death the majority of people are "earthbound", staying close to the earth of their own choice for many reasons. Some do not even realize they have passed through death and remain around the home and family, often going to work as usual and wondering why no one speaks to them or pays the least attention. This is especially true when it has been a sudden death like a fatal accident. Puzzled and bewildered, the deceased may finally suspect what has happened or be met by an inner-plane Helper — someone who has already crossed over and has been trained in rescuing these souls. We asked some of these earthbound entities if anyone had come to meet them and the majority said no, they saw no one. However, a few affirmed that they had seen a figure in light who was beckoning to them but they were afraid and would not venture near.

In the time of Jesus, during the history of the early church and into the middle ages, possession by devils or demons was well known and exorcism was a common practice. It is even mentioned in the ancient records of the Greeks and Egyptians. However, discarnate attachments or symptoms of possession or demonic influence are more prevalent now than ever before. This, we understand, is due to changes in frequency of the protecting "veil" between the Astral planes and the Etheric-physical. Not only are the earth frequencies being speeded up but also those of the human bodies so that it appears to be much easier for a discarnate entity to attach to a human aura or enter inside than it was seventy-five or a hundred years ago. Because the veil is now so thin, it also facilitates contact with those who have passed through death, as many clairvoyants and trance mediums have attested.

There are many books written on after-death experiences so we will only say that if a person has lived a good, moral life according to the best of his knowledge, he will usually be met by a Light Being. Often a beloved relative or friend who has preceded him will come and he will be taken to his proper level computed by the soul. There is never any mistake about this as the soul knows exactly where the entity belongs. He may go through a dark tunnel at the moment of death, but there is a light at the end where his loved one or angel awaits.

Those who have been heavy drinkers, smokers, or strongly addicted to drugs or any habit, carry the tendencies or desires with them and after death, these desires are often so intense that the entities attach themselves to living people in order to enjoy those habits vicariously. They frequent places where people of like habits are gathered so they can enjoy their habits through them and then enter a body at the first opportunity and are often unaware that the body is not theirs! People on drugs are especially surrounded and possessed by discarnate entities (hereafter we will

2

call them "D.E.s") who were drug addicts, and also illicit or perverted sex practices draw them as well. A single individual has often been found to have as many as sixty or seventy D.E.s attached to his aura.

Usually the first sign of entity attachment is a feeling of extreme fatigue or of being drained, often with a strange or heavy sensation in the solar plexus. This may or may not level off as the body adjusts to the foreign entity or entities.

Another common symptom is a strong body odor — very unpleasant and usually nauseating. One woman wrote us that her husband had developed a putrid, nauseating body odor after he had been in an automobile accident and hospitalized. She and other family members could hardly stand to be around him. We found that D.E.s had come in during the accident and were both inside and outside the aura. A release was done for him, and afterwards she wrote in gratitude that the odor on him had vanished, but had remained on his clothes. She had to send everything to the cleaners while he was on a business trip.

Another woman asked us to check her sister, a minister's wife, who had developed a nauseating body odor after a stay in the hospital. She too had D.E.s attached to her aura and after the release, the odor left immediately and it was a pleasure to be near her.

Odors of this kind are not carried by all D.E.s, only certain ones.

Another sign, especially of possession, is a strange look in the eyes. This may include protruding eyeballs or an emptiness, a dead look with no life or sparkle to them.

Besides having little energy and feeling drained all the time, there is the opposite symptom of having too much energy or showing extreme nervousness. Hyper-active children nearly always are found to have D.E. attachments.

A sudden change in personality after an operation or accident is another sign of possession, as well as most epilepsy and schizophrenia. This is explained in Chapter 17.

Another common symptom of D.E. attachment is a constant feeling of anger, animosity or hatred toward everybody and everything for no apparent reason. There are many other symptoms of D.E. attachment but these are a few of the most

3

common ones.

We shall now describe the activity of these attachments in the realm of frequency. Without physical bodies, entities are energy frequencies – the lower the consciousness of the entity, the lower the rate of vibration. "Are they not pure light?" people have asked. No, they are not, for one does not become pure light until he reaches the very high celestial realms, far beyond the astral planes. These D.E.s are still functioning in their astral bodies. True, they can move through a wall or other inanimate objects as they are not restricted by the solidity of the purely material world, but *man is a living soul!* Man is soul and spirit encased in a physical body as well as an etheric body, an astral or emotional body, and a mental body. These are called the "Four Lower Bodies" and they are all surrounded, for protection, by an electro-magnetic force-field called an aura, and science now corroborates this.

When a person dies, it is only the physical body that is lost. This body is for use only on the physical plane, like a coat or garment of chemical matter which is discarded when the soul leaves and it is no longer needed.

The other three bodies function as follows: The etheric body, which extends an inch or more out from the physical and is made of much finer substance, has two parts – the lower etheric which is the exact duplicate of the physical body and also disintegrates after death, and the higher etheric body which is the soul body, in which the soul functions in the spirit realms.

The astral or emotional body is next and this remains for quite a period of time after death and then gradually disintegrates. It is slightly luminous and surrounds the physical body in an egg shape; also, it is the "feeling" body in which one perceives all emotions – love, joy, hate, anger, etc. This is the body that the earthbound entities use, as well as those that are in the astral planes.

The mental body, we are told, is of a soft golden, luminous substance surrounding the head. Although this body eventually disintegrates, the *mind* itself is part of God and never dies. This remains with the part of consciousness that is waiting to reincarnate. When a soul is ready to reincarnate, it must first go to the mental plane to pick up a mental body, then to the astral plane for an emotional body, then to the etheric plane to receive material

4

for an etheric body, and finally into the new physical baby body. However, the earthbound soul retains its bodies until it decides to reincarnate or is removed.

Those less evolved D.E.s who are not earthbound are drawn to the lower astral planes where they torment themselves with desires that are never gratified. They stay there until they have the desire for something better and are then taken to a higher level where they can be taught and prepared for a more favorable life on earth during their next incarnation. It is said that spiritual beings often visit these lower planes, speaking to these souls and trying to induce them to repent and come up higher.

Time will be taken here to briefly mention suicides. Those who take their own life do nothing to benefit their condition, no matter what the reasons. As we understand it, one who commits suicide is earthbound and stays in the same situation, still overwhelmed by the same problems, although he can do nothing to solve them without a body. He stays in rather a suspended state until his natural time for death arrives, and then he may go on to the astral plane. However, God is just and there are some with terminal illnesses who have taken their lives so as not to be a burden on their loved ones or because the pain was more than they could bear. This is taken into account by the soul.

Our Father God has provided safeguards for man, one of which is the aura that usually serves as a ring-pass-not, unless the frequency is lowered to that of the surrounding discarnates. Then, through the vibratory attraction, these D.E.s are clamped on — in most cases, on the outside of the aura. This does not mean that discarnates can pass through embodied individuals at will. *They cannot.* For example, if a physical body sits in a chair which a discarnate entity has chosen to fill, the D.E. does not enter the physical body. Both are occupying the same space on different rates of frequency, so there is no mingling of the densities.

Earthbound entities are nearly always of a very low moral caliber, in fact, extremely so. In the early days of our training, we used to interview some of them, with the aid of a pendulum. (See Chapter 4.)

In one case, we questioned two D.E.s, the first of which informed us he had been an alcoholic and chain smoker with a violent temper. His language was vile and he had abused his wife and children. In addition, he was a professional thief and had been convicted of armed robbery.

The second D. E. let us know he had committed several murders and landed in a penal institution. He also had been afflicted with violent headaches and had died of a cerebral hemorrhage.

Three D.E.s were interviewed in the case of Mr. W. in which two were female. One woman had been a heavy drinker of alcohol with lowest morals and language – a real guttertype, but she blamed God for all her misfortunes.

The second woman had died of lung cancer. She had been a cleaning woman and the fumes from the strong solutions she used had irritated her lungs. She was extremely nervous and had a sharp, cruel tongue.

An over-bearing man with a severe temper was the third D.E., and he admitted to mistreating his wife and children. His death had been caused by a heart attack.

Mrs. W. had also requested a release, and the D.E.s with her were quite different in that they were all relatives and none particularly evil. The first was a grandmother on her father's side who didn't even know she was dead! The second was a cousin we did not take the time to interview, and the third was her mother, a very domineering type. They all left very willingly.

After a few weeks of interviewing D.E.s, during which we found that nearly all of them were in the category of thieves, drunkards, murderers, drug addicts or sex maniacs and the like, we decided to curtail this part of the analysis as it was too time consuming and really served no purpose.

On the other hand, we did learn that some D.E.s stayed around the home just to be near the family or because they did not know where else to go. Often in great grief and despondency, the bereaved one would draw the deceased mother, husband, wife or child into their aura. This powerful, magnetic energy keeps the deceased one from going on and he often becomes attached to the aura. Occasionally someone will ask us to check to see if a certain deceased relative or friend is around them as they often have felt their presence.

It is important to know, however, that the more highly evolved souls that are not earthbound can also make their presence felt. They are as close as a thought and can feel our love and prayers for them wherever they are in the "many mansions".

The greatest service you can do for friends and relatives who are dead or dying is to pray for them. Pray that they will be met by a trained "helper" who will guide them to the level where they belong. Also remember that dead loved ones – so-called dead – are very much alive and can benefit from your prayers, especially if earthbound. The Douay (Catholic) translation of the Bible informs us: "It is well and good to pray for the dead." But this was deleted from the King James version.

Many clairvoyants can see the D.E.s on the outside of an aura. For many years we were privileged to attend a group in which love, peace, and harmony were sent to the world and some release work was also done. Katherine, leader of the group, as well as some of the members, could see the spiritual beings working with us as well as negative discarnates.

One morning the request was made that we work for the husband of one of the members. His personality had suddenly changed and he had begun drinking heavily (only an occasional beer before), swearing, and becoming violently angry over the least little thing. He was also seeing another woman!

Our angelic helpers brought the husband into the middle of the room in his astral body. Katherine could see three very evil faces attached to him and they communicated with her telepathically. One had been a driver of a horse and buggy, cursing and beating his horses; the other had been a drunkard, constantly demanding more whiskey, and the third was a very flouncy woman who had been a prostitute. After the release was complete and they were removed by our Indian helpers in the spirit realm, he improved.

Another morning, Katherine informed us that a great Being had come striding into the room, wrapped from head to foot in a huge cloak of white material. As she watched him, she noted that his white robe was tinged with gray; there was something strange and she had an odd feeling, so she challenged him in the Name of the Christ. Suddenly he flung back his cloak and stood there revealing a defiant figure dressed in a tight black suit, his cloak lined in red. Throwing up his arms, he shouted, "I challenge you to touch me, I dare you!"

We were told he was a former black magician, and while he stood there, smiling sardonically, we began calling for the Light and for the In-God-We-Trust Angels who came in with a large net of golden light which they threw over him. Then they pulled the cord and carried him away, kicking and screaming! Most people have thought, from childhood, that when a person dies he goes to heaven or hell. Actually, the majority stay earthbound. One could call the lower astral realm "hell" and the higher astral realms, "heaven", but it is the opinion of many leaders that we make our own heaven or hell right here on earth. However, the astral plane around the earth is made up of seven levels with many sub-levels, the lower levels being places where the most evil entities are drawn. If it is a hell, these entities make it so by their own vicious thoughts and feelings.

The middle astral levels draw the bulk of ordinary people who have not been especially bad or good. This level is called "Devachan" in the esoteric writings, and we understand that these entities often mentally create the same homes and surroundings that they had on earth, with mental images of their loved ones – as often they don't even realize their bodies are dead.

To the Fifth Plane or level gravitate the souls that have begun to search for the light – those from various religions or those who have sought to help their fellow man and lift themselves to a higher degree. It is possible to reincarnate from the Fifth Plane.

We do not know much about the Sixth Plane except that souls do not incarnate from it. This is apparently a training center where they learn and prepare to go on to the next plane, from which they can reincarnate. It is sometimes called a "door" to the Seventh Plane.

The Seventh Plane is the highest plane of the astral realm and here are found many of the great souls of earth – the teachers, philosophers, spiritual leaders, and scientists – provided, of course, that they have lived exemplary lives. The soul, as we mentioned, always computes itself to the level to which it belongs. Of course, there are higher levels of consciousness beyond the astral which we will not discuss as they have no bearing on our subject.

The writer has been in several groups where a trance channel was able to bring through the voices of earthbound entities, and they were released by the efforts of the group and spirit helpers. One woman was asked why she had come in to our group, and she replied wistfully,

"I smelled the coffee and mmmm – it smelled so good!"

Then there were others who claimed they had just been floating around from one place to another, not knowing where to go. When asked if they were aware of their physical death, some were not and this fact was explained to them. We then called in the spirit helpers who would lead them away to the plane where they belonged.

In a similar group to the one mentioned above, much to everyone's surprise, several Christian ministers came through, and when asked why they had not gone on to "heaven", they claimed they were afraid of the hell-fire and brimstone they had preached about, feeling that it was just possible they might be taken there!

It was very interesting to learn that there are hospitals in the etheric realm where the etheric and astral bodies can be healed and revitalized in cases of a long illness where these bodies have been depleted. Also, when a person has been burned to death in a fire, he can be taken to one of these hospitals. The victim may be in a comatose state long after death and the soul must rebuild the etheric and astral bodies whose material is subject to damage by fire.

To any actors or actresses who may be reading this, please consider the following from Dana N., who wrote:

"About a year ago I began work on a project which changed my life. I am an actress – the project was a stage production of Medea in which I played the sorceress, Medea. The end result was a thrilling evening of theatre which nevertheless lost money and destroyed relationships. For me, personally, the experience was bizarre and frightening as well as one of growth as an actor.

"Medea is part human, part god. When her man betrays her, she uses her dark power to kill the other woman. She then murders her children to free them from him forever. My particular approach to my work probes the unconscious to express aspects of my own psyche that are analogous to the character. This requires internalizing the feelings – 'living' the role."

An analysis showed that Dana had eight D.E.s of a very negative nature, inside and outside the aura, and they were affecting her emotionally as well as physically as most of them had come in during Medea, although a few had been there before. There were also demonic thoughtforms with her and all of this negativity had succeeded in lowering her wisdom and spiritual levels. She was cleared of all the above and given a restoration period of about ninety days. A year later Dana wrote, "Thank you for your help in the past. Alter the clearing I have continued to say the prayer you sent. Also, I have worked again. The play was successful; I was pleased with my efforts for the most part, and I did not have the problems I had with Medea."

In a personal experience, the writer played in "Gaslight" the part of Mrs. Manningham whose husband was trying to drive her insane or at least make her think she was going mad. We played the part intensely and felt ill during the rehearsal period and all the performances. Our director comforted us by saying that every actress he had known, playing that part, had become ill while doing it!

It is very important that actors playing negative roles, do not let their own inner feelings become involved. This is very difficult to do — to play a role truthfully and become the part on the outside, and yet remain detached from it on the inside. The basic self must be made to realize that this is only a play and it must not affect the solar plexus area (where most D.E.s enter). Besides saying a prayer of protection before every rehearsal and performance, one should visualize a cross of blue-white flame in front of the solar plexus and then put himself in a circle and tube of white Christ light. Doing this before going to sleep at night is also a must.

It is the opinion of those who have labored for many years in release work, that our earthplane is loaded with hordes and hordes of D.E.s — that they are everywhere, and one should constantly keep himself protected. Happily, we also know there are many helpers in the spirit realms who have volunteered to meet the souls of the newly dead and we understand our earthly father is one of them. But those who are already earthbound desperately need assistance and there are some teams and groups who are now doing this.

CHAPTER 2

Causes Of Discarnate Attachments

Although vibrations of the aura are easily lowered through drugs, alcohol, and other vices, it is more often through EMOTION. Anger, temper tantrums, feelings of great depression or rejection, or even extreme fatigue or hysteria can lower the auric frequency. In fact, any uncontrolled emotion changes the auric field and draws to that person D.E.s of like nature, and this is one of the reasons self-discipline is so important. This is why the Masters of the ages have constantly stressed that one must learn to control one's emotions and thoughts. A person who lets his emotions control him is like a wagon hitched to a team of runaway horses. *We have the God-Power to control and discipline the lower self – now we must use it.*

Every time a feeling of anger, hate, jealousy, greed, etc. just begins to be felt – take charge of it, transmute it by immediately replacing it with a detached feeling or better yet, with *love.* You may call for "Light", "Help", "Jesus", or any Divine source, but do not express these feelings, for this is only feeding them and giving them momentum. One soon loses complete control, not to mention the hurt it causes loved ones and others. Neither should these feelings be suppressed and harbored inside for deep negative feelings in the subconscious are the cause of many diseases, both mental and physical. They must be forgiven, changed and transmuted.

All bars are frequented by throngs of D.E.s vainly trying to get a drink, having discovered they can't even hold a glass without a physical body! But they can assimilate the odor and emanations.

11

Hopefully, they await a chance to enter someone's aura and really enjoy the same sensations the body feels. Some clairvoyants have actually seen this happen. One man, who was visiting a bar for research purposes, could see that all empty space up to the ceiling was crammed with desperate faces. He began to watch a certain man who appeared quite inebriated, and as he continued to drink, his aura just suddenly opened up! Then to his amazement, three or four of these hideous creatures immediately pushed their way in. As the aura closed again, several more D.E.s attached like suction cups to the outside. The man then staggered out of the door.

Our friend looked around and could see the auras of other people opening up also and D.E.s rushing to get in.

We must remember that the D.E.s that hang around a heavy drinker are generally dark energies of a very low level. If they have not actually attached to him, they will often follow him home and stay there, affecting his thinking, self-esteem, and that of others in the household. The personal connection to his divinity or Higher Self is also weakened and in time, actually blocked.

The Bulgarian Master Omraam Mikhael Aivanhov has quite a bit to say about evil discarnates in his book, "Life"[1], page 107.

"As human beings are completely ignorant of what takes place in the invisible world, they don't know either what the sentiments or thoughts are that attract undesirables and repel luminous entities or inversely – and without knowing it, they attract dark and injurious entities. Within us, around us, everything is full of malevolent entities and those who are sensitive are appalled by it. They smell odors and feel currents which make them very ill at ease."

He goes on to say on page 144: "One mustn't introduce impurities in one's thoughts and sentiments for they attract the inferior spirits which will come and install themselves to be fed... When man is evil, jealous, envious and assailed by all sorts of covetousness, his aura immediately shows gaps, flaws and cracks through which the undesirables insinuate themselves."

Again Aivanhov says that man's vices such as the heavy use of alcohol, tobacco, gambling, etc. "are made up of beings that the man must feed because he invited them and has so strengthened them that he is completely dominated by them and cannot get rid of these forces."

We must say here that our work, per se, is not for the evil ones who would only attract more D.E.s anyway. This release work is primarily for the spiritually awakened people and their families who have unknowingly attracted discarnate entities.

It is so important that we learn to become impersonal, to detach from hatred, anger, resentment, selfishness and greed, and learn to replace these feelings with love. Not loving the evil others have done to us, but impersonally loving the real self of the other person; for how can we judge others when only God can see into their hearts and motives?

The apostle Paul said: "Dearly beloved, avenge not yourselves, but rather give place unto wrath: for it is written, vengeance is mine; I will repay, saith the Lord." Rom. 12:13.

This is difficult to do and takes practice, and as we cannot accomplish it alone, we must have the help of our Heavenly Father.

As we mentioned before, after death, an angel or spiritual guide is always available to help and guide the deceased if one is aware. All one has to do is look for the light and go into it. But man has free will and there are many, who because of fear of going to hell or a desire to enjoy their old habits vicariously through embodied individuals, refuse to leave. Some just prefer to stay around their former home and possessions, although they do not necessarily attach to anyone. Often their presence is felt and it is said the house is "haunted". Especially if a person has been murdered, he will often remain at the scene in his astral body, sometimes for hundreds of years. Those who suffer a violent death often stay in the building or area trying to call attention to themselves and see that the crime is discovered and avenged.

Most ghosts are simply the astral bodies of people who have lost their physical bodies, although some are thoughtforms clothed in filmy astral substance that disintegrate in time.

D.E.s can wind themselves around a victim, draining his energy and life force, causing great trauma to the unsuspecting victim. Often the entity does not realize he is harming the person, sometimes a loved one. A doting or bossy parent may stay around a grown child and try to manipulate him just as he or she did in the physical. Even a loving parent can be earthbound, held by the extreme grief of the children; and conversely, a deceased child can be held by the distraught parents.   And if the aura of one is particularly weak or open, the loving D.E. can become attached through no fault of his own. He just came too close! Then again, some do not realize what they are doing as they are trying so desperately to cling to life as they knew it.

CHAPTER 3

Kinds Of Attachments

Entities Outside The Aura

When there are D.E.s outside a person's aura, they cling to it like suction cups and they cannot get free. This is the area of least influence and is usually indicated by unusual fatigue, outbursts of temper, frequent headaches or nausea. One sometimes notes a strange fluttery feeling at the solar plexus; and there are other symptoms too, but these are the most common.

When the vibratory frequency of one's aura is lowered to the frequency of the surrounding D.E.s, they can attach. Then as the vibrations are raised to normal, they find themselves locked in or "stuck" there.

There is usually a period of from twenty-four to forty-eight hours after a release when one may experience many kinds of trauma. Some people go on crying jags after the work has been done. For example, Patti cried for three days after her release. On Monday she had cried the last two periods at school, the last two or three periods on Tuesday, and the last four on Wednesday! The next day was a good day with no crying. She didn't know why she was crying any of those times. Since then, her mother reported, she felt good.

Judy wrote, after she received our letter, that at the very time of release, she was driving her car and suddenly burst into tears. She had to pull over to the curb and sobbed and sobbed. At the time she did not realize what was wrong — until she received our letter several days later.

✧ ✧ ✧

When Marlene wrote for help, she had already requested a release for her husband and son, who had shown great improvement. She said she had been under severe stress since early spring and believed she was under some kind of negative influence. When she took a picture of her son to send to us, she felt strange, and said:

"Until I mailed the envelope something was trying to take me over and make me forget the whole thing and also do everything wrong. You wouldn't believe everything that happened. The influence was so strong it took everything I could put together to write it and mail it."

She also added that they had stayed for several weeks, while visiting in another city, in a house where they had some very weird experiences and they had not felt right since.

This family was very spiritually oriented and working actively in the Light. Marlene had seven spiritual guides and her High Self was in good contact. But she had three D.E.s outside the aura that were affecting her emotionally. The home, however, was clear. She wrote back after the work was complete:

"When I closed my eyes to go to sleep, there was so much light I couldn't sleep. It was like a huge light shining on me and it was warm. My husband asked me what I was doing. He said when he shut his eyes, he saw light! I told him I wasn't doing anything, which was true. Later I felt two (D.E.s) lift off the top of my head or at least they released at the top of my head. Then I felt one loosen from my back and then release, and that one was painful. However, I know when that one entered. It was at a football game last fall and it felt like someone stabbed me in the back. It went right in next to my shoulder blade in the back on my left side. I think it was affecting my heart and my health. Anyway, it is gone!

"For about three days, all I've wanted to do is sleep, and then my body started throwing off a lot of debris. After the release, I saw brilliant lights of all colors — it was like the 4th of July. I thank you very much. I am feeling better and thinking much more clearly."

✧ ✧ ✧

Sally was a lovely girl of fifteen, but had suddenly become pale and sickly-looking. She had spells of nausea and faintness, usually in church. One Sunday, her mother rushed out of church with her, before the communion services, because she was sick to her stomach.

We were told that her mother had recently remarried to a man who turned out to be cruel, stingy, and became furious when they went to church. She felt she had made a grievous error in marrying him three years before.

We found that there were sixteen D.E.s with Sally, outside the aura, and there were thirtyeight in the home. After Sally's release, there were no more of the symptoms, and her stepfather changed completely after a release had been requested for him.

✧ ✧ ✧

We found six D.E.s with Lucy, outside the aura, and fifteen in the home. She wrote after the release:

"Your letter to me said you did my work August 20 in the morning. That afternoon, I was driving from Texas to Kansas. I was aware of strange little surges within me – like little nameless fears and shocks. They made me catch my breath several times. I was sure at the time that you were doing the work.

"I also began to see things – my problems – in a different light that day. I made some decisions and gained a new perspective. And I've gained a greater sense of my own worth. Thank you. I know my life will be better now."

ENTITIES INSIDE AND OUTSIDE THE AURA

When discarnate entities are found inside the aura, there are nearly always some outside also. In only one or two instances we have found them inside the aura exclusively and that was when they had already received partial assistance from someone else.

Entry inside the aura is usually made through a break or crack in the aura, or it can be damaged through intake of mind-expanding drugs or alcohol. Some writers call this an "obsession", however, in our work we call it an obsession when one is possessed by an idea, fantasy or thoughtform. (See Webster's New World Dictionary)

Clairvoyants have told us they can see actual holes or tears in auras and of course, D.E.s could enter very easily. They can also come in when one is deeply under an anaesthetic or momentarily unconscious from a blow or fall. We strongly urge everyone about to be given an anaesthetic to put themselves in a circle and tube of White Christ Light and call to the angels for protection.Strong emotional outbursts like anger can open up the aura. At such times, being "beside one's self with rage", or "out of your mind" or "blowing your top" are quite true. At such times the aura is opened to the point that D.E.s can enter or at least be attached. Therefore, we are urged to practice control of thoughts and feelings. After the D.E.s have entered, the temper tantrums or extreme sexual desires or any uncontrollable appetites get worse and worse and open the way for more D.E.s to enter.

Actually, there is not a great deal of difference in symptoms whether the D.E.s are inside or outside the aura — it is in the degree of penetration. D.E.s can attach through all the means we have mentioned in both categories depending upon the state of the aura.

Before a release is begun, it is necessary to make an analysis of the individual situation, and certain measurements are made with the aid of a pendulum over the person's picture or a handwriting sample. We are able, in this way, to pick up the individual's vibration and we ask to contact his High Self and Guardian Angel for the desired information.

First, however, we say a prayer for protection and divine guidance, asking our High Self for permission to do this work. In a very few cases, permission has been denied as the Higher Intelligence sees that the person would not profit by the work and would only attract more D.E.s and possibly be worse off than before.

After permission is given, we ask if the High Self is in good contact as it is often blocked; also, how many Spiritual Guides are with him. Then we take a plus or minus reading on the conscious and subconscious levels; if minus, it indicates there are D.E. attachments, if plus, the person is clear. We inquire as to the number of D.E.s and the depth of infiltration, and whether the D.E.s are affecting the host mentally, emotionally, or physically.

The depth of inner stress is determined on a numbered scale in which 324 is normal — anything above this indicates the amount of stress caused by the friction between the D.E.s and the real self. These measurements are all taken before and after a release so we can determine the depth of the negative influence.

A character reading is also taken and this is also on a numbered scale, but in this case, the higher the number the more developed the character. Readings are also taken on self-evaluation, willpower, and determination which are shown on the basis of average, below average, or above average. If the client has seven or more spiritual guides, we take an evaluation of his wisdom and spiritual understanding. If less than seven guides, he would not have developed much in this area. There are also other measurements taken but these will be discussed in later chapters.

✧ ✧ ✧

Mrs. R. L. wrote us: "I first became aware of the presence of outside entities back at the beginning of March of this year when I received an 'energy transference' (unbeknown to me) and was suddenly opened up to some psychic energy. For approximately two months I was controlled by a community of astral beings who led me to believe I would take shortcuts on the Path if I obeyed them." (Note: There are no shortcuts!)

Mrs. L. had been given a reading by a psychic healer and was told that she had had an incredible 'rebirthing' at which time most of these beings could no longer reach her. However, there were still some negative energies hanging around. Mrs. L. said she continued to hear one or two voices, and she also asked that their house and two-acre property be cleared.

Our analysis showed that there were eighteen D.E.s inside and outside the aura, affecting her emotionally and physically, and there were twenty-six in the home and premises. After the release, inner stress came down one hundred and two points to normal but the other measurements were not drastically affected, although they came up. Character was above average and went up seven points. Wisdom increased six points and her spiritual level, which was already high, went up eleven more points. There was a sixty-day restoration period.

Mrs. L. replied immediately, "I got your very exciting letter today. Bless you for your releasing work! It seems too good to be true. I just hope it lasts and that I do not attract any new personalities." Apparently she did not as there was no further request.

From time to time we have received a request from someone

who is clairvoyant and can actually "see" as well as feel the attached discarnate entities or spiritual helpers who are near. It is so rewarding to have someone confirm and verify what we pick up only with a pendulum and intuition.

✧ ✧ ✧

Liz P. wrote, "I have been bothered for the past two years by a spirit. Sometimes at night it will try to possess me and only through will power and a very strong faith in God and His assistance has it been kept at bay. I sometimes become so weak during the encounter that I physically want to give up. However, intellectually I know that if I stop fighting, I'll awaken a maniac. So the fight goes on. Lately... he is being joined by others. I can see a parasitic blackness on the left side of my neck in the aura. It is interfering with my circulation for I am cold most of the time ... When I intend to do something spiritual to any degree – talking to someone, meditating, writing you – I begin to shake as if I were very nervous. My jaw becomes rigid and tonight my throat felt strange, as if someone else was there wanting to scream at me in a great rage."

When the analysis was made, we found that Liz had forty-seven D.E.s, some inside the aura and some outside, plus a partial possession. There was also an "open psychic door" at the base of the skull. These were all effecting her emotionally and physically. The entity described above was, or course, the possessing force which we referred to as "Number One", there were so many.

After the release, the above symptoms were gone but it took several sessions to completely clear her. Liz's aura was so damaged that other forces were able to come in, but as the aura healed and strengthened and she learned to protect herself better, she remained free.

Liz wrote, "You asked how I felt? I had just told my brother yesterday at lunch that I felt better, as if you might be working on me!"

Then she went on to list the events since release: "Last Sunday (three days before the release), I was very low energywise and moralewise – really on the bottom. As I said in my letter, you were my last chance. Since I was tired, I tried to take a nap. My neck was bothering me so I decided to try to communicate with

20

the entity (Number One) and he did respond. He ranted and raged at me. I forgave him for trying to harm me and said even if he killed me he would never get control. I also said I loved him and that blew his mind completely. There was some kind of explosion inside my head and my right ear popped loudly but I was able to sleep. The rest of the week is a blur. All I can remember is being tired and strained, and seeing auras especially well after Wednesday (the day the release was done). Also, I have been much more perceptive of entities, and seeing auras, future events, etc.

"One thing bothers me. On Friday night, two days later, I went to Yoga class and while going into meditation, I was totally distracted by a sensation like a knife being held in the right side of my neck near the collarbone! I had the impression it was another entity — one I hadn't encountered before. I don't know if that would be some of the debris you mentioned or not, but I just got the impression he was there to let me know it's not over yet." (We rechecked later and there were indeed more D.E.s attached, and another release was performed.)

Liz went on to mention some of her background and it is interesting that two of the people in her life were into some form of black magic.

She told us that, "This entity, which by the way gained possession around the beginning of September when I had a horrible row with my brother and was knocked down... and really was on the verge of insanity. Also, I think 'Number One' and I met in college through a girl named R.L. If there is such a thing as a carrier, she was."

A deep love affair the next year was described but it ended by his having to marry someone else — "trauma after trauma and many tears", she continued. "I'd never try to take my own life but often prayed that I'd die. That's when 'Number One' used to smother or hit me. The sister of this guy I loved was also into black magic so I may have gotten too close to some of her entities also. All of this had to happen, I'm sure, and with every event I've grown that much faster."

Next Liz reported that since the releases, she had felt more comfortable inside and out and had been able to sleep better also. She said she felt "healthy, happy and more rested, especially in the past two days."

Then a wonderful, glowing letter arrived: "Thank you for the song in my heart. You've helped to return to it. I've noticed that through the songs, these entities sneak in also, especially Rock. I've stopped listening to the radio, I only try to listen to the song within." Liz had enclosed some pictures she had painted to explain more fully what had happened during the exorcism, and described them as follows:

"This is the media I've been using to self-analyze. The lines and colors show thought-forms. These are uncolored. I did the first the week you did the exorcism and the other about a week before. In both pictures, the left side of the figure seems tortured or pleading with its open arms, and the word 'we' seems to indicate many intruders and as you can see, they are within the aura."

We had found the psychic door at the back of her head open and she referred to this with an interesting experience. Before her first letter to us, she had attended a class on psychic healing.

"When I got home", she continued, "I lay down on the floor to examine my 'self'. I asked for God's protection and help and then began. Three shining figures were present, two at my feet and one at my head. There was a shadow over me and I asked that they help me remove it. The two figures at my feet each held the shadow on my feet. As I forgave myself for the things that came into mind, they were able to lift the shadow off. In spots it would stick and then we'd have to work hard to free myself from the shadow. Also, in places there were scars and blisters which we healed with coaching and direction from the figure at my head. Things went rather progressively until we got to the base of the skull in back of the head. There the shadow went inside and all through my body. It was like a network of roots. Well, we tried, but I got exhausted before the whole thing could be removed... I noticed that that area was just as you said, quite open."

It is truly gratifying to have corroboration for our work from those who are aware and can "see". This particular entity had entered her open psychic door where it may have been "based". Normally, there is a doorkeeper, an elemental being, assigned to keep one's door closed. Occasionally, however, the little elemental gets bored with its job and leaves and the psychic door can be opened by means of a fall or blow, or even too much practice in the psychic field such as automatic writing or extreme psychic exercises.

The shadow that had entered through Liz's open door was removed, the debris cleaned out and the door closed. We requested her Guardian Angel to contact the elemental kingdom and ask for a new doorkeeper to be assigned to Liz to keep the door closed. This was accomplished.

This unusual young lady had great insight and spiritual understanding. She wrote later that, "While I was pondering a problem I was having, I came to the realization that if I didn't want to feel stressful or frustrated, I shouldn't let those feelings in. So I have been practicing a sort of detachment and have found myself more comfortable inside and out and have been able to sleep better also. Thank you again. The answers are always there when we need them. 'Ask and ye shall receive.'"

Liz kept in touch with us for quite some time. Within a year she met a wonderful young man whom she married, and a year or two later they announced the birth of a beautiful baby boy and sent us his picture.

❖ ❖ ❖

Bette wrote asking for help in clearing negative energies from her life and also her apartment, and especially in breaking a very destructive relationship of which she couldn't seem to let go. Then she mentioned a very large stuffed panda bear she owned – a psychic friend had detected a negative being inside of it. She had burned incense but wasn't sure it had helped.

Our analysis showed twenty D.E.s inside and outside the aura which were affecting her emotionally and physically. There were also twelve entities in her apartment, but the panda was clear! Also, her spiritual guides had been blocked but were found to be in good contact after the release was completed.

Bette replied three weeks later but mentioned neither the panda nor the unhappy relationship; however, her beautiful letter was very rewarding.

She said in part, "On May 1st (the day after her release), I was aware of a profound change in my energy level. I noticed I had more energy than I have had in many years and it has been pretty much maintained even though I'm expending probably two to four times as much energy because I'm doing so much more... I

23

have noticed that my thoughts are so much more positive and continue so! The inner feeling of calm is very evident and I find I can maintain inner peace to a much greater extent, no matter what people do externally. I also feel such a burden has been lifted and somehow I feel more clear and focused... And my apartment feels 'lighter' and more open and spacious. I really feel that April 30/May 1 was a turning point in my whole life!! I wanted to thank you from the bottom of my heart. Bless you and your healing work. I have recommended you to a friend in crisis who has noticed the change in me. By the way, everyone I have seen or talked to by phone has told me that I seem so much happier."

Nearly a year and a half later, Bette wrote again saying that for several months she had been on a downward spiral of deep depression that she couldn't shake.

She added, "I'm constantly depressed. All the activities that once brought enthusiasm and fun are dull. I'm unhappy in all aspects of my life and I'm continually tired no matter how much rest or sleep I get."

Our analysis showed that more D.E.s had attached outside the aura, but her home was clear. All of the symptoms she expressed are very indicative of the presence of discarnate entities. A release was performed and we heard no more.

✧ ✧ ✧

Carrie was a Light worker who was helping many people, but she felt she was fighting forces that were overwhelming her. We did indeed find D.E.s outside her aura, a few inside too. After the release, she wrote:

"The change is almost unbelievable. People – many – have commented that they no longer pick up bad feelings from me, that my face has lost its hard look and even lines, and that I'm looking radiant. Inwardly, the confusion is leaving, many things I've had to fight are ceasing to be a problem and my communication is becoming better. For the first time in my life I'm free from worry and am able to live on total faith – confident that all will be well regardless of how things may look at times.

"And even material things are better and for once it looks like they're on the upswing. I guess for me the best thing of all is now there's an inner knowing that I can and will do the things I've been told I came to do – all doubts and fears are gone. I have a self-confidence I have never before possessed and it's all so fantastic. I'm even able to send the Light much better, and when doing massages, I'm able to 'turn on' my hands to a much greater degree. By that I mean I can dissipate energy blocks for well over an hour without them (hands) ever really tiring."

✧ ✧ ✧

Joyce had D.E.s inside and outside the aura, taking a great deal of energy and causing fatigue. She said the request had been sent by her husband without her knowledge.

"But I knew immediately", she wrote, "that something incredible had happened to me by the way I felt, so light and free and able to breathe again. I had felt drained and fatigued, both mentally and physically. However, the day after the release, I felt a strong upsurge of physical energy and mental well-being. In this last week, my self-confidence and sense of inner solidity have grown steadily, as has my energy, efficiency and all-around enjoyment of daily activity."

✧ ✧ ✧

Nearly everyone who has had a release through us, has also had D.E.s in their home. In fact, many people who have recently moved, will ask to have the new apartment or home cleared. D.E.s can be left by former tenants or they can be brought to one's home along with workmen or even people visiting!

These are stray entities who are not attached to anyone but tend to linger around those whose vibrations they like. For instance, if they crave cigarettes, they will be drawn to someone who is smoking, or drinking if they crave liquor – or anything else that appeals to them. Odors may draw them, some perfumes like musk. Other odors repel D.E.s – "Seabreeze" and eucalyptus oil are two, and it is said that iodine repulses them – just two drops in a small glass of water will keep the room clear.

In doing any kind of release, we always check the home and clear it. We call on the angels of the Violet Flame to sweep through the building, dissolving and consuming all negative energy that might be in the floors, ceilings or walls, after our helpers have removed the D.E.s. Then we ask that the home he filled with light and love.

We have even been asked to check an automobile, where indeed D.E.s have been found and removed.

PARTIAL POSSESSION

What we call a partial possession is when the invading entity and the conscious self are both inside the body fighting each other for control. Each wants to be in authority and sometimes the D.E. is in the driver's seat and at other times the real self is in control. This is quite obvious to observers as they will notice a change in personality and actions at times, and during other periods, the person will seem like himself. Of course, whether in a complete possession or a partial possession, there are nearly always D.E.s inside and outside the aura as well.

When Benji's mother wrote to us for help, she was at her wit's end trying to cope with this seven-year-old who had had such a drastic personality change over a period of three years.

Seventeen D.E.s were found inside and outside the aura, but also a partial possession inside the physical body. It seemed to have happened about three years previously, but we were never told what had occurred at that time.

After the release the mother wrote, "My son Benji had improved greatly and was back to normal before I ever received your letter. He is truly a very bright child — spoiled, yes, but before you helped him there was a drastic change in his personality. He is very much back to normal."

✧   ✧   ✧

It is seldom that we have received such detailed information, either before or after a release, so we are pleased to include this story from Gordon's mother, Joan P., and a family friend.

Gordon, a thirteen-year-old boy was in serious trouble which had started about two years previously. At that time he was involved with a boy whom the mother felt was under demonic influence. But at that time she was very ill, too ill to cope with his actions and sudden personality change. So he and his sister, Ann, went to spend the summer with their father and Gordon stayed on for the school year.

Joan said that prior to the personality change, Gordon was a joy and wonder — liked by everyone and he seemed to enjoy his life and friends, as well as his mother and her friends. Also, he was fascinated with the mystical world.

During the school year with his father, Mr. P. phoned Joan

several times and was beside himself as to what was going on. He had left a woman friend with Gordon while he went out of town for the weekend and Gordon drove her away. She was a psychologist and had then written Mr. P. a long letter describing Gordon's behavior and how disturbed he was. Also, Gordon would pull weird tricks on his father's friends, male and female, to shock and embarrass them. One woman told him that Gordon was another "Damien" and was possessed with evil.

When Gordon returned to his mother, who had by then recovered, she realized how much worse he had become. Gordon wasn't nice to anyone – he insulted Ann's friends to their faces and on the phone, calling them every horrible thing imaginable. He and Ann were fighting constantly to the point that the neighbors called the police three times. He would not cooperate, and became violent and insulting when asked to do anything.

"His insults were precise and horrible", we were told, "drilling straight to the core of his victims". He would not go anywhere but just sat at home watching television, and he craved sweets, which was excessive. Also, Gordon would take brooms, ice skates, baseball bats and tennis balls and try to attack Ann and his mother, becoming unusually strong at these times. A frightening look would come over his face, an evil look in his eyes, and his face would twist in anger – he was totally out of control.

Gordon only went to school because the juvenile officer from the police department talked to him and made some headway. His mother said, "When I picked him up at school or took him there, he hid down in the seat so none of the kids would see him. He had lots of friends before he left, but when he returned would have nothing to do with them. They came up to him and said things like, 'Aren't you Gordon P.? My goodness, you have changed!'

"Teachers couldn't help, he was obstinate with them. I talked to all his teachers, plus the principal, plus four school psychologists and they said they couldn't get Gordon to talk, that he seemed very angry and uptight like a bomb ready to go off. Everyone who met him at this time told me how disturbed and dangerous he was. His personality had changed completely."

When we were asked to help Gordon, his analysis showed a partial possession with seventeen other D.E.s inside and outside the aura. Conscious and subconscious levels were extremely low, minus twenty on our scale, which indicated the possessing entity was extremely evil and in full control although the "real" Gordon was still in his body. Of course, this D.E. refused to leave, being fully convinced it was "his" body.

In cases where a D.E. refuses to leave with our helpers, we call for a special band, the In-God-We Trust Angels, who come in with a net of golden light in which they place the reluctant entity or entities and carry them off by force.

Gordon's possessing entity was taken in this way, and the other seventeen had gone willingly. A restoration period of ninety days was indicated and it was necessary to work with him four times during that interval because his aura was so damaged that it was easy for several D.E.s to attach on the outside when his energy was low or he felt depressed.

However, the results were fantastic – immediately! His mother wrote ecstatically, "Since he has been cleared, there has been a complete change in every respect...He is doing brilliantly in school just this past week, and all his teachers are congratulating him. He isn't defiant to the students and teachers as he was before. He is mixing with the students now and he told me he felt happier.

"During that bad period, he had run up a large amount on his charge account at TN (boys' shop) and today he got the bill and was so depressed. He said he didn't deserve all those clothes – or any breaks – that I couldn't afford to pay for extra things while I was trying to get my business going! His entire attitude has changed about everything. There is no more hostility or anger and he is looking forward to going to school and bringing his grades up... He does whatever I ask him to do around the house and is very affectionate to me –we have wonderful conversations about lots of things. He reads to me and does his homework nightly – which never happened before without a battle. He is considerate of others and isn't insulting Ann and her friends now. That warped, angry expression is off his face and out of his eyes, and he can be reasoned with.

Anyway, his present condition is the way he was before – sweet, considerate, polite, and interested in things and people. He's bright and open-minded.

"What an experience! Thank God you have been able to help him because I really don't know how much longer I could have taken it. I am extremely grateful for your returning Gordon to us."

It is interesting that after seeing a movie on Possession, Gordon said that he felt that had been his problem! Also, in doing our analysis, we picked up a great deal of drug residue in his body. His mother was stunned at the idea of drugs and said that he had no time for anyone who used drugs, smoked, or drank liquor, and that he had been a loner since the change in personality.

Gordon absolutely denied ever taking drugs. A mutual friend and counselor for Mrs. P. also picked up the drug vibration and that he had sniffed cocaine while at his father's. She asked, "Is it possible that both of us were picking up the vibrations of the possessing entity and not Gordon?"

Indeed it is possible and highly probable. If the entity had been into drugs before his death, he would still retain the essence of the drugs he had used as well as the craving for them. If Gordon had had the opportunity, the entity undoubtedly would have caused this craving to be fulfilled.

COMPLETE POSSESSION

A possession or "complete possession", as we use the term, is when only the D.E. is in the physical body, possessing it, while the real self or consciousness has been thrown out of the body into the aura. It is inside the aura like an alien entity! In order for this to occur, a tremendous force is needed such as takes place in a hard fall, blow on the head, or a severe automobile accident. This can also take place during a traumatic birth.

In a release of this type the switch must be made instantaneously, and we ask our spirit helpers to remove the controlling D.E. and replace the true self. This takes much prayer and energy, sometimes requiring two or three release sessions before the changeover actually takes place. We also call to the angels of the Violet Flame to sweep through the four lower bodies and dissolve and transmute the negative energy and thought patterns or habits left by the departed entity.

❖ ❖ ❖

Candy was a high school teenager who had been giving her mother nothing but trouble and we were asked to do a release for her. The analysis showed a complete possession here, as well as D.E.s inside and outside the aura, and three of them had come in

29

at birth. Candy's Higher Self was barely in contact and she had no spiritual guides. However, after the release we found the High Self to be in good contact and she was given five spiritual guides. Her mother wrote that it was not the same at their house – Candy had become a bright, loving girl – and no back talk! The mother had been out in a storm and Candy was actually worried! Two months ago she would have been out drunk all night, we were told. At school, Candy was not as loud in the hall and she was actually studying in the lunch room, her teacher reported. The mother said she did not even look like the same child.

❖ ❖ ❖

Joe was sixteen years old when his mother wrote us for help. He had had problems from birth and always had to be rocked to sleep. When he was six weeks old, he had a strep infection and was treated with weekly shots of Gamma Globulin for a year. At the age of four, he started brandishing butcher knives at his mother and sister and was put on Ritalin for several years. At the time of writing, he was diagnosed as hyperactive or hyperkinetic. He had a very low boredom tolerance and was a junk food addict as well as a T.V. addict. For eight years he had been in institutions – a mental hospital, a home for boys, and a detention home among others. When the release was requested, Joe was in a military academy because of needed discipline. His father had died when he was seven.

Our analysis showed that Joe had extremely low conscious and subconscious levels; his spiritual guides were blocked as well as the High Self. There was a complete possession plus fourteen D.E.s inside and outside the aura, so Joe was not even in his physical body but was inside the aura like a D.E. The entity in the body had complete control.

Seven D.E.s had come in at birth, including the possessing entity, and his psychic door at the base of the skull was open.

A release was done for Joe; in fact it took two sessions as the next day it was found that four D.E.s had refused to leave and two new ones had stepped in. His psychic door was closed and sealed.

It was felt intuitively, while working, that Joe had been a Nazi under Hitler in his last life. It seemed he was unwillingly so, had been forced into it, and that was why he was allowed to embody in the United States. But he had deep feelings of frustration and hostility to work out.

The restoration period was four months and it was quite amazing what took place during that time. Three weeks after the work had been done, he had gone to live with his sister who had curtailed his junk food addiction. He still watched T.V. all night and slept all day, as this was during the summer. When school started, his mother reported that he was acting better and seemed more at ease with himself. He was playing football at the military academy he attended. She said he didn't steal, take drugs or alcohol.

By Christmas, her report was ecstatic: 'Joe is doing so well I can hardly believe it. He was made First Sergeant of his company, is a 'star' at football, and is unbeaten at wrestling."

And so another life was salvaged by the power of God through release!

❖ ❖ ❖

Another similar case was that of Chris. When his mother wrote us, he was nine years old, hyperactive, deeply disturbed, and on Ritalin. He was found to have eleven D.E.s inside and outside the aura and also a Possession that had entered the physical body at birth. We picked up that he had also been a Nazi soldier or was possessed by one. (These were our only two cases on record).

Chris' mother wrote a few days after the release:

"I have suspected he was a Nazi pilot for several years, to the point that I have mentioned it to several of my friends and to my two oldest children, both of whom agreed with me. When Chris was about six, he wrote a letter to the boy next door, saying, 'I like you even if you are Jewish.' Since he had never heard such ideas at home and they had to come from somewhere, I started thinking then in terms of a Nazi incarnation in his last life. Several times since then he has made disparaging remarks (about Jews).

"Around a year ago we were discussing what his (astrological) chart showed as the best career for him. When I suggested he might be a pilot, his reaction was specific and emphatic, 'NO! The floor of the airplane might catch on fire and burn my feet.' (Incidentally...he was born with a slight foot deformity.) He is inordinately interested in war, reads all he can about it and draws countless pictures of crashing airplanes... He watches reruns of Hogan's Heroes nightly and frequently jumps up, extends his arm

Nazi-fashion and shouts, 'Achtung!'.

Just last night he told me, 'Hitler was a brave man.' His chart quite clearly shows experiences with black magic in past lives. I know that the nine and a half years of his life have been sheer hell and I pray that he has already worked through much of his destructive karma and can find peace."

A month later she wrote, "Chris is doing beautifully. The change he has made borders on the miraculous. He's much calmer, he's doing better at school, and he's a joy at home. He even made a negative statement about Hitler last week! We have cut his Ritalin in half and plan to eliminate it entirely after tomorrow."

❖ ❖ ❖

George was described to us as a "strict teetotaler" of Crow Indian and white descent, and was adopted as a child. He hated women and alienated everyone who tried to be his friend. At the time his name was sent in he was a transient who had just been evicted from the last shack in which he had lived and was living in a tent in the cold northwest, seemingly unable to do anything about his situation. A neighbor, who was trying to help him, sent his name to us as a last resort!

Our analysis showed extremely low conscious and subconscious levels, twenty-five minus, which was practically nil. His High Self was blocked and there were no spiritual guides, and we found a complete possession, as well as thirtyone other D.E.s inside and outside the aura. They were affecting him mentally and emotionally, as well as physically and were taking a great deal of energy. Character measurements were also extremely low, almost to the point of a moron. It was necessary to do two releases over a period of three days but our final recheck showed him to be clear and the true self was back in the body functioning.

Inner Stress went down two hundred and thirteen points to average. But surprisingly, character went up seventy points to above average, showing the extremely low functioning level of the possessing D.E. Self Evaluation was still below average, but willpower and determination had come up to average.

It was two years before we had any news of George, at which time his benefactor wrote to say that George had come to call on him for the first time. He did say that after he had received our letter that the exorcism was complete, he had gone to see George,

32

who was not home. But he left the release information where he could find it and heard no more.

In this letter he wrote: "I had invited George to stop over a number of times in the past years but realized that he probably would not because he was very mistrusting of everyone's intentions. When I saw George walking to my door, I knew he had changed; he never would have come if he hadn't changed. I invited him in and was anxious to learn what he had experienced, but he volunteered nothing; he just talked pleasantly – and that was unusual. George listened when I talked and he never used to listen.

After an hour of this conversation, I felt confident enough to ask him how things went about the time of his exorcism. He admitted that he had quite a traumatic experience, but didn't dwell on it. He needed a bath desperately and I offered him the use of my shower... He accepted and I was soon to learn just how much he had changed. His clothes were extremely dirty and I offered him a change of underwear. With that he replied that he already had more of my clothes than he deserved. (I had given him a bunch of clothes when he had no money to buy any and his were in shreds.) He had accepted them, showing little gratitude, but his comment now showed me there was a beautiful person there that I had never known before. He turned down my offer of a change of clothes and I understood that his real self was emerging and I had to let him do it his way.

"We started to get into the process of exorcism at which time I gave him a copy of your 'The Healing Ministry of Release' sheet, which he read over and seemed to understand most of it... His understanding of metaphysics is far in depth compared to the average person's. He wants to know more, so I suggested he stop in Peggy's place. He indicated that he may go see her and that represents another drastic change in his personality because he never had any time for women before.

"I am sending you this dialogue because I'd like you to know that your ministry has, once again, shown meaning in accordance with God's Will and I am sure that you will be justly rewarded for your work. You have helped to save a life that I have seen the evidence of."

✧ ✧ ✧

Mrs. J. had a grown son, Ken, who caused her a great deal of worry and concern. She told us that he had had a bad fall from his bicycle when he was fourteen and had not been the same since. His personality had changed completely from that of a cheerful, happy and loving boy to that of a morose, arrogant and sardonic stranger. He had a brilliant mind but could not get along with people – no one liked him, although he was married at the time.

We offered to do a release for him as we had checked and found there was a complete possession, but his mother refused to have anything done for fear it might be "dangerous", and that it would be better to "let well enough alone".

DISCARNATE ENTITIES IN THE HOME AND ENVIRONMENT

Seldom do we find a home or building that is completely clear of D.E.s as there are so many, many ways that they can be drawn to a home, office, hospital or even a school. As we mentioned earlier, a discarnate entity will often stay on in the house after his death, considering it to be still "his" home. Then, the new tenants may bring more D.E.s with them, and some of them will stay on regardless of how many more tenants come and go. This explains so-called haunted houses and ghostly noises.

However, in haunted houses, the ghostly or discarnate occupants usually deliberately make their presence known by such manifestations as cold drafts, creaking stairs when no one is using them, cupboard doors swinging open and slamming shut by themselves, and other unusual demonstrations.

Of course, there are poltergeists which we will take up in a later chapter. They often cause objects to appear and disappear and love to play pranks.

One would not expect discarnate entities to hang around hospitals, but they do. They especially stay in the maternity sections where they try to enter the body when a baby is born. Normally this is not possible, but when the child's aura has been weakened by a long, difficult birth or the mother has been given too much anaesthetic, one or more entities may enter the body. This can be prevented by adequate prayer and protection for mother and child both before and during delivery.

There are also "carriers", people who constantly draw negative D.E.s and are apt to leave a few wherever they go, especially if the D.E. prefers the new place!

❖ ❖ ❖

Mrs. M. had to have her septic tank pumped out, and upon its completion the man in charge came in the house to be paid. After he left, she noticed a strange feeling about the room — an intangible but very depressing sensation which she could not explain. Suddenly she thought of the possibility of D.E.s having come in with the septic tank man, and immediately began to call to the angels and Indian runners to come in and clear the house. (She had some training.) As she prayed and visualized the violet flame throughout the house, the strange vibrations left and the energy in the room was lifted and lightened.

D.E.s are often drawn to vile odors and anyone working in that environment would be apt to draw them.

❖ ❖ ❖

We were asked to clear a dormitory room on a college campus where a young lady was living. Apparently there had been drug activity in that room as it was loaded with entities. But as we worked, we were impressed to ask for a release for the entire campus. Then our assistant, who was often clairvoyant, exclaimed that the Indian runners had spread a huge net across the campus, several holding it at each end, and others were throwing the D.E.s into the net by the hundreds! When all of the dark shapes had been placed in the net, they pulled it together and carried them off.

Cemeteries and old battle grounds are always in need of clearing as D.E.s often stay around the former body until it has disintegrated. Whenever we pass a cemetery, we always call to our Indian helpers to come in and take the D.E.s into the light where they belong.

Clairvoyants tell us that over many old battlegrounds, the soldiers are still fighting in the ethers, unaware that they are no longer in physical bodies, thus setting up a vortex of very negative energy that can be felt throughout the whole area.

Kellogg Hill near Covina, California is divided by a freeway and for years there were many accidents at the particular spot, for no apparent reason. A friend of ours lived over the hill and said they heard so many crashes and were often awakened during the night by the sound of yet another accident.

She asked if we would work on it, which we did in our group. It was found that this was the site of an ancient battleground and the enemies were still engaged in combat. Shortly after we had called in our Indian runners to clear them out, our friend excitedly reported that they had been aware of no more accidents at that spot.

A member of Katherine's group in the early days was a retired Colonel who felt it to be his unique calling to travel through the south, visiting all the Civil War cemeteries and calling for the release of the discarnate soldiers who didn't know the war was over! When he returned, he related that as he walked up the path to one of the graveyards, the negative energy was so powerful that he was knocked down by an invisible force and fell flat on the ground! It took him a few minutes to build up a positive frequency to counteract it.

One should be aware that it is also possible for D.E.s to be attached to objects, especially things they have loved or created.

Several times we have mentioned Katherine's class in which we were trained. She always sat in a certain chair, a very old circular chair from France which was said to be almost two hundred years old. There were always several in the group who could channel by voice, including Katherine. One morning, during the early days of her work, a man's voice came through with a decided French accent, informing them that his name was Dupierre and that was "his" chair Katherine was sitting in. He went on to say that he had designed and built the chair, and after his death had remained with it. He realized now that he should not be earthbound and asked to be freed. So a release was done for him, and also for a female discarnate who came into the group asking for a release. She said her name was Inez.

To the delighted surprise of the group, about six months later both Dupierre and Inez spoke through one of the channels saying that they had requested permission to come back and help in freeing discarnates. This had been granted to them and for the past six months they had been in training, on the inner planes, for this work. From then on, whenever a release was to be performed by the class, after calling for the Indian runners, Lone Wolf and Mighty Waterfall, they always added, "and Dupierre and Inez".

They were a distinct benefit to the work as they could talk to the D.E.s who could see them, and help to persuade them to go into the Light. An interesting note is that soon after our work by mail was begun, Dupierre and Inez went on to higher levels of progression to prepare for another earthly life.

The writer has a special interest in Chinese artifacts and a few years ago was given a very old Chinese drum, about twelve inches in diameter. It was charming but we felt odd about touching it and gingerly set it up on the fireplace mantel. When we happened to be near, there was an almost malicious emanation felt. Suddenly we realized that possibly the former owner was still attached to it. This turned out to be the case, and although he was a musician, had been an evil and conniving man. After we explained that he could ask forgiveness and be taken to a place of progression, he willingly left with our helpers. Needless to say, we had a completely different feeling about the drum and began to enjoy the beauty of the craftsmanship as well as the red and green dragons painted on its surface.

CHAPTER 4

Use Of The Pendulum

The question has been asked as to how we determine the number of discarnate entities present, the depth of infiltration, and other measurements. The answer is that all of these are done with the aid of a pendulum, which is the most accurate method we have found. Even a clairvoyant can only "see" the entities outside the aura and can only guess at possible deeper levels of attachment.

A pendulum can be any small object like a button, bead, or ring which can be threaded with a silk or nylon thread or very light chain. There are also many ready-made pendulums available that are made of wood, metal, plastic or sometimes crystal. For our work, we do not recommend crystal because it is extremely sensitive and can pick up negative energy and store it. We prefer a light metal instrument with a sharp needle-like point in order to swing directly over the lines on the charts we use.

Dowsing, divining, or detecting all seem to apply to the use of a pendulum and it is called radionics when applied to health. There are two kinds of pendulum movement; one is an oscillation or back-and-forth swing in a straight line. The other is a gyration or circular movement – clockwise for "yes" and counterclockwise for "no".

There are several different ideas about what causes the movements of a pendulum and the best way to use one. Most of these methods can be accurate if the subconscious mind is trained accordingly.

There is nothing "witchy" about using a pendulum any more

than a thermometer or blood pressure equipment. We are taking measurements by tuning in to the body intelligence which swings the pendulum, and to the higher mind for accurate answers.

The dedicated couple who trained us in using a pendulum as well as their release ritual, stressed the importance of a high level of consciousness, living a clean life, and becoming well acquainted with one's basic self. This basic self is the body elemental which controls all of the unconscious functions of the body – like the beating of the heart, breathing, digestion and elimination, growth and health of the cells, and so on. The Rosicrucians call it the "Body Engineer". It is this basic self that must be loved and understood, and trained to give correct answers through the swing of the pendulum. For convenience, he is given a name, often George[2]. Ours is Chris.

He or she (sometimes the female is dominant) must learn to accept only that which comes from the High Self, not you, the consciousness. The basic self wants to please you and at first, will give you answers that he thinks you want. The operator, who holds the pendulum, must learn to remain calm and unemotional, completely detached. He must hold no thoughts of his own – what the answer might be or what he would like it to be. The period of training is longer for some than others and one must be constantly testing, "Is this information coming from the High Self? Are you sure?"

Test him at first with questions regarding subjects about which you are acquainted and know the answers to. When he can answer correctly, then introduce him to your High Self and teach him to ACCEPT ONLY THAT WHICH COMES FROM THE HIGH SELF.

The basic self uses the subconscious mind just as our "middle self" or consciousness uses the brain mind. In order for the conscious mind to receive an answer from the High Self, the contact must be through the basic self. We were given a diagram once which helped to explain. It was of three rectangles on top of each other, like three stories of a building. The bottom space represented the subconscious mind, the middle space was the conscious self, and the top space was the superconscious or High Self. In order for a message to get from the High Self to the conscious self, it MUST go by way of the subconscious mind, used by the basic self. So, in working with the pendulum to receive correct answers from the High Self, the basic self is trained to get his answers from the High Self only and pass them on to you.

The best pendulum book we know of is, *How to Use a Pendulum* (please see Bibliography). It was compiled by a doctor who prefers to remain anonymous and was written by his nurse, Stella Askew. He brings out the fact that the pendulum is a very sensitive instrument and "is greatly influenced by the planets and other invisible forces and influences." Although most of his work was in the field of medical diagnosis and foods and does not pertain to our work, still there are most important facts that are generally appropriate.

In order to obtain the very highest results possible, one should always begin work by holding the pendulum in front of him or (as we were taught) over the knuckle of the first finger of the left hand, if right-handed. If left-handed, over the right hand. Then ask, "Pendulum, are you in harmony with me?" If so, one should get large clockwise gyrations or circles, indicating this is a favorable period. If anything else is received such as small, cramped circles, counterclockwise circles or any discouraging movements, wait about thirty minutes and try again.

The doctor notes that there is a period of twenty-four minutes in every two hours when a pendulum may not answer correctly. This theory is based on cycles of time called "Tattwas", part of a Yogic science. He has proven this theory and so have we and others. As one's basic self becomes trained, the pendulum will always give counterclockwise circles if it is a negative period. But often, right in the middle of testing, the pendulum movements will become erratic, making elliptical movements, jerky motions, or even stop altogether. Immediately take the pendulum off of the testing material and hold it over the knuckle, asking silently, "Pendulum, are you in harmony with me?" You will be sure to get a negative reply, so just wait and do something else for at least thirty minutes.

We feel that this twenty-four minute period in every two hours, when a pendulum will not give correct answers, is when the electromagnetic field of the body is recharging itself, although this is not brought out in the book. We have found many times, that right in the middle of an analysis, the pendulum will start contradicting itself, or give impossible or unlikely answers. We then stop and check and sure enough, we are entering a negative time period!

There are several other necessary precautions when doing an analysis for release work:

1. Always remove all jewelry other than gold, especially one's watch. This can have a detrimental magnetic effect on the pendulum.

2. Say a prayer of protection: "Father-Mother God, I surround myself and the pendulum in a tube of blazing White Light of the Christ, and I ask for perfect protection, reception, and that only that which is truth shall come through."

There are times when the pendulum will hardly move or acts strangely, even though it is in harmony. Ask if there is interference as sometimes an invisible force will try to control or manipulate the pendulum. If it swings, "Yes", call for the angels of the Violet Flame to sweep through the interference and dissolve and consume it with the POWER OF LIGHT! Then check again; if it still swings negative, rephrase the question. Sometimes the question is not quite understood by the basic self and should be asked again in a different way. Ask, "Do you understand the question?"

3. One must raise his consciousness up to the level of the High Self as we must stay out of the psychic realm, which is in the astral level. There we find discarnates that are destructive, or pranksters and imposters who don't know any more than we know — or not as much. We say the prayer, beginning at the heart center and going up to the top of the head:

"Father-Mother God, I raise my consciousness UP into my Higher Self of spiritual knowing", and keep the mind stationed there.

4. It is absolutely necessary to learn to be DETACHED and IMPERSONAL. We can influence the pendulum, as well as others around us, by thoughts and preconceived notions. By being completely detached with our consciousness centered at the top of the head, we are open to intuitive flashes from our High Self.

Last of all, we would advise no one to try to use a pendulum without first reading the two books already mentioned: HOW TO USE A PENDULUM by Stella Askew, and THE SECRET SCIENCE

AT WORK by Max Freedom Long.

In taking our measurements to find out certain necessary information, we first place the applicant's picture or handwriting over an open Bible with our little chart over it. A photo of any age is o.k. but handwriting must be in ink. We first, of course, check to see if the pendulum is in good harmony, and then say the prayer of protection. Then we attune ourselves to our High Self and Guardian Angel, asking for permission to do a release for the applicant. If the answer is affirmative, we then proceed to ask if the High Self is in good contact and how many spiritual guides the person has. One just beginning on the spiritual path usually has five guides, as well as church-goers and other good moral people.

In our work, we have found that the uneven numbers usually refer to spiritual work and the even numbers to the mundane.

We do not consider numbers below five as those people would have no interest in anything of a spiritual nature.

Five – symbolizes a five-pointed star and usually suggests freedom of choice, with reference to life plan. One can live a mundane life and just pay off karma or he can make an effort in the study of truth and the search for fulfillment of soul. As one progresses, he can always be given more guides, if needed.

Six. – suggests the six-pointed star or the double triangle, the blending of spirit and matter, or reaching up for the spiritual and bringing it down into everyday life. This often takes a creative form of expression like art, music, or writing, etc.

Seven – denotes a mission, the lightworkers number. They may not know their mission, but will be guided to it in time.

Eight – this number suggests balance – "As above, so below – as below, so above". This person is achieving balance in his life and usually excels in the business and financial areas of life as well as becoming spiritually oriented.

Nine – a special mission. These people have come into life for a certain spiritual mission – ministry, healing, including medicine. As the number seven begins to achieve his mission, he is often given two more guides. In fact, anyone can receive more guides if they are needed.

Ten – this denotes scientific ability to a high degree.

Eleven – another kind of special mission. These people are usually in healing, release work, or other spiritual leadership.

Twelve — we have had no examples — probably very high scientific and spiritual ability. A Nicola Tesla would come in this category.

Thirteen — this is the highest number one can have, the most anyone needs. It is the symbol of twelve plus one, as Jesus and the twelve disciples or the sun and twelve signs of the zodiac. Some world-famous spiritual leaders have thirteen guides as well as other not-so-famous devotees who work in the silence.

If necessary, at any number, the whole band of guides can change as they go on in their advancement and others that are more suited to the person's needs, take over.

We then ask for the conscious and subconscious levels. If the pendulum swings to the minus side of the chart, we know there are negative attachments. If to the plus side, the person is clear.

We then ask how many D.E.s there are present. To determine this, we count slowly until the pendulum reverses, but confirmation is requested from the guardian angel. Whether there is a possession or partial possession is then determined, and how many entities are inside and outside the aura. Also, we ask if the home is invaded and how many are there.

It is important to find out if there are any supraphysical shells (astral) from a past life, and then check for a possible mind control, hex, spell, curse, or implant. (These will all be explained in later chapters.)

We find out then if the D.E.s were giving the applicant mental problems, emotional, or physical problems as well as what is the degree of inner stress? This is the amount of stress built up between the real self and the invading D.E.s. Normally, stress measures 324.

The numbered scale we use is very similar to Dr. Brunler's Biometric Analysis, which is a scale of 1 – 1000. First, we measure character for which 324 is average for a good, moral person. For the "man on the street" it is 321 or less. Most of our applicants fall in the category of 324 to the upper 400s after a release. The exception is for inner stress, this should be no more than 324. When it is higher, it shows how much stress the D.E.s are causing.

We have been asked what we mean by "character" in the measurements taken for an analysis. It entails how we meet the problems of daily living – life, death, suffering, misfortune, as well as the nagging little perplexities and inharmonious personalities. How do we discipline ourselves? And are we wise enough to take the circumstances that are thrust upon us and utilize them to our advantage? In other words, can we turn the stumbling blocks into stepping stones? Nothing molds character like discipline, and how much we can discipline ourselves and yet look on the mistakes of others with tolerance, without judgment, is another yardstick of character. A test for self-evaluation is done next. Is it below average, average, or above average? Average is the only acceptable answer as below average would denote an inferiority complex, and above average would indicate an inflated ego. Often either of these is caused by the invading D.E.s and will return to average after the release.

There is a "psychic door" at the base of the skull which should be kept closed and guarded by a good doorkeeper (an elemental). If the door is open, (often through an accident or severe blow on the head), D.E.s can walk in and out.

If a person has seven or more spiritual guides, the wisdom and spiritual levels are determined. We consider "wisdom" to indicate how a person is *using* his spiritual understanding in everyday life. This is also on the scale of 324 (average) to 1000.

The day after the release, all the measurements are taken again to show where the D.E.s were influencing the most.

Last of all, after the release is complete and we have determined that the person is completely clear of all D.E.s and negative influences, we ask how long the restoration period will be? It usually takes between thirty and ninety days for the inner bodies to return to a normal pattern. The D.E.s leave debris which must be purged and it takes time, especially if they have been there long, with certain patterns and habits established. Restoration is like programming a computer and during this period one can be helped by prayer, meditation, and affirmations on one's own part or from another. Remember, one must be willing to change himself, his thoughts and habits for a release to effect permanent change.

Dr. Herb Puryear made a profound statement in a lecture we heard, speaking of one's willingness to change himself. He said, "When any individual makes a change, God has to reprogram the

Universe!" What a mind-boggling thought! This behooves each one to make some decision about what needs to be changed in one's life, and then follow through on it.

Finally, it is important to remember that the pendulum can be an accurate guideline but it should never be considered infallible. Receiving correct answers depends on several criteria: (1) The degree of cooperation of the basic self and its training. (2) Making sure that the basic self is in good harmony by checking the left knuckle. (3) The spiritual evolvement of the operator. It is said in the book, HOW TO USE A PENDULUM that "The pendulum will never give reliable answers if the operator does not follow a clean life... and cooperate with the Maker in every way to better life situations."

As one becomes closer to his High Self and continually works with the basic self in love and understanding, the answers become ever more reliable.

One must never take every answer from the pendulum as gospel truth, as many neophytes do. If it does not "feel" right or coincide with what one already knows or is way out of line with what one feels is a logical answer, *Rephrase the question.* For instance, one may ask how many D.E.s are with a certain person and count up to seventy or eighty before the pendulum changes its swing. If the person had fairly high conscious and subconscious levels, one would know this was not possible. So one must keep training and working with the basic self, emphasizing that it MUST get its answers from the High Self.

Say, "George, you are not giving me a correct answer. Please check again and tell me the truth."

If he comes up with six or ten D.E.s, you know this is more like it. But keep questioning, "Is six correct? Do you confirm this with the High Self?"

The training period may take a year or two, but it is well worth it.

We also warn against using the pendulum for ordinary personal problems in lieu of making one's own decisions and learning and growing thereby. To rely on a pendulum to determine "Is it going to rain today?" or "Should I sell my property in East Hoboken?" is really tempting the basic self to just tell you what it thinks will please you. The High Self usually does not interfere in mundane activities. However, when one is in a spiritual quandary or dilemma, it is safe to ask, first making sure that the basic self is in good contact with the High Self.

Many times operators use a pendulum for checking food as to chemical additives and positive or negative qualities with excellent results, also for medical diagnosis. But this is a different field entirely.

CHAPTER 5

Children

Children are very often infiltrated with D.E.s. They generally come in at birth when the mother has been deeply anaesthetized and/or has had a long hard labor. Accidents also temporarily open the aura and many children have had bad falls or blows on the head, even as babies. Most cases of hyperactivity and related problems, as well as epilepsy, are the results of influence by discarnate entities that are possessing the body.

Glenn was eleven years old and hyperactive, with problems of hostility and fear of people, when his mother wrote us. He was even afraid of people he knew! His pediatrician had him on Ritalin and Dexedrine, with no improvement.

Our analysis revealed a complete possession at birth plus other D.E.s inside and outside the aura, blockage of the High Self, and an absence of spiritual guides. There were also sixty-two D.E.s in the home. Incidentally, his mother said she was a heavy drinker and later requested a release for herself.

After the release was completed, his inner stress, which had been extremely high, came down two hundred and fifty points to almost normal. There were only four points to go during the restoration period of ninety days.

Glenn's mother wrote, "Words are not adequate to thank you for what you have done for Glenn. I noticed a change in him last week. Even though you didn't finish on him until midmorning of June 4, he seemed different at breakfast. He has seemed more calm and peaceful."

Nearly two months after the release, his counselor phoned

47

us to say that Glenn's improvement was amazing! He used to hide from people and wouldn't talk. Now he came over and chatted with the counselor and showed him his models. He had also been hostile to his mother's affection, but now went up and threw his arms around her!

A year later his mother wrote, "As a mother who knows her child well, you will understand when I tell you that the progress Glenn has made in a year is just miraculous. He still has his moments, but the evil and destruction are gone. We were especially gratified to get his school report in May and see how much he had climbed this year in his tests. His jumps on tests (with the freeing of his mind) were fantastic. I am so thankful to God every day for this freeing of my child so that he may grow into his proper potential."

A month after Glenn's release, the whole family was checked and cleared. The mother wrote that about ten days after her work had been done, she began to notice that she wasn't drinking anymore! Maybe an occasional glass of wine with dinner, but the old desire to drink was GONE! She also wrote later that she had overcome an "awful fear of death that I wrote you about."

Glenn is now a fine young man and joined the Air Force when he was eighteen.

✧ ✧ ✧

Jimmy's mother wrote us when he was seven, saying he had had birth problems, vomiting his own blood from birth to five days old. At five months, he had a temperature of 106° for three days. Later, behavior manifested in headbanging, undistinguishable speech (later developed), and other behavior diagnosed as "early childhood Schizophrenia" which he seemed to have gotten over.

Though she said Jimmy was an "exceptionally sweet, bright, sensitive child whose affection and even friendship were offered with an open heart", he would often try to hurt his younger brother. Also when asked to do something he did not want to do, he would start an ugly, hateful screaming for up to four hours or more... During the fits of rage, his body would often convulse and he would experience much physical pain in his arms, legs, and abdomen, as well as splitting headaches, all of which would tend to disappear when he returned to normal. He seemed intent on hurting the house, his toys, and himself during these episodes.

Our analysis showed a deep infiltration of very low entities inside the physical body, also inside and outside the aura. They had come in at birth and age five months. Jimmy had three spiritual guides and his High Self was in contact so they were helping as much as possible. After a fit of rage, he would seem surprised and say, "I don't know why I even started it." After hurting his little brother, he would look bewildered and then filled with grief, he would sometimes cry louder than his brother!

It took two release sessions to complete the work as three D.E.s refused to leave and the angels took them by force. Jimmy's mother said he experienced a slight headache and nausea the next day and day after. The following day, Jimmy said to his mother, "I feel like a different person. Do I look different?" He also reported that he was no longer afraid to sleep in his room.

Billy was a twelve-year-old whose mother asked for a routine check for D.E.s. We found that two had entered the body at birth, plus many inside and outside the aura. There were D.E.s as well in his grandmother's home where he was living. However, he had seven spiritual guides which indicated his soul had come in to complete a spiritual mission.

After the release was completed, Billy's mother reported that forty-eight hours after the release, her mother had phoned. (She knew nothing of the work that had been done.) "She was concerned about Billy as he had started running a low-grade temperature and had an upset stomach, and she wanted to know if it was all right if she took him into the hospital should the need arise. He continued at the same level until late Saturday afternoon (forty-eight hours). As there was no worsening, she had only called the doctor, but his prescription wouldn't stay down and had only made him feel worse. I called her late Saturday evening and she could not imagine why, but he felt so bad he couldn't sleep until after dinnertime, then for some reason he went in to lie down and was out like a light. Around 8:00 p.m. he woke up, after two and a half hours sound sleep, and was without temperature and ate like it was his last meal! She said she couldn't understand it, but she was so amazed because it also seemed as though there were some changes in the child that she couldn't put her finger on but she could see it in his person. Or, she said maybe she had been absent-minded and had not noticed some attitudes about him before. I want you to know that this is the first time in my life that I've known her not to observe or be aware of something!

"Case closed and a life reopened. Thank you."

We have found so often in our work that the immediate results of a release seem to be nausea, with vomiting and headaches, especially when D.E.s are inside the body or inside the aura.

✧ ✧ ✧

Peter's mother wrote to ask for a "release of some sort of demon that is possessing my child." She said he was six years old and had disturbing personality characteristics, explaining:

"He is unable to stand pressure in school in testing situations; has a fear that no one likes him; is very self-conscious about freckles; is extremely selfish and greedy, and generally lacks self-confidence. Lately I am becoming disturbed by his rejection of God and any form of religious instruction."

She noted that he had had a very difficult birth.

We found extreme problems – a complete possession at birth plus other D.E.s inside and outside the aura. Although his High Self was blocked, he had seven spiritual guides which indicated a spiritual potential.

Three years later his mother wrote, "Peter is doing just fine and I must tell you he is a most delightful, loving child. In the past year we have had many changes in our lives, but Peter is growing at a rapid rate on a very spiritual level."

Three more years after this she wrote again, "I must report he's (Peter) growing into a fine young man – twelve years old, seventh grade, and an excellent student and a very spiritually-developing young man, full of love. Thanks to you and the Spirit of the Universe."

She also mentioned her parents for whom releases had been done. "I'm happy to report their lives are very different now. I visited them in the spring and it was the happiest time I've ever had with them. My father is like a person I've never known – happy, loving, supportive, thankful for all he has and is very content. I've never seen this before. My Mom was great too. Of course, she has a whole new life now too."

✧ ✧ ✧

We have found that all children we have tested, who were diagnosed hyperkinetic (abnormally increased muscular movement), have had discarnate entities attached to them.

When the name of Jerry was sent to us for work, he was described as a "difficult child – a hyperkinetic child with a perceptual-motor problem and and also somewhat under-nourished in a family with plenty." He was ten years old at the time and his handwriting looked rather infantile. One relative whom he visited called him "impossible."

Our analysis showed that the High Self was blocked, although he had four spiritual guides. There were eighteen D.E.s inside and outside the aura, including a complete possession in the body at birth. After the release was completed, there was a necessary restoration period of three months. During this time there was a dramatic improvement. However, the family continued to request rechecks at nine month to two-year intervals. We found during this time that his "psychic door"at the base of the skull was open and his doorkeeper was not adequate. (We did not know about this psychic door at the beginning of our work).

In most people, this psychic opening or door is closed and guarded by an elemental doorkeeper. We called on our healing angels to close this door and seal it. Then we asked Jerry's guardian angel to send to the elemental kingdom for a new doorkeeper, one who was properly trained to keep that door closed.

When the psychic door is open and unguarded, D.E.s can enter and leave at will. This seemed to be Jerry's problem after the first release as every time we checked him, he had a few D.E.s outside his aura. After his "door" was closed, we checked one more time over two years later and that was the last time. Jerry graduated from high school and went on to college. He is now happily studying in Europe.

✧ ✧ ✧

Tim had been a very difficult child from birth. At age twelve, his mother wrote that he was extremely negative and she felt he needed release work.

In checking him, we found nine D.E.s, some inside the physical and some inside the aura – they had all come in at birth and felt that Tim's body was their's. His spiritual guides were completely blocked, although the High Self was in contact. After the release, there were two D.E.s left that refused to leave. Another clearing was done and the In-God-We-Trust angels took them off in their golden nets. He checked clear the next day, but we felt there were some nutritional problems — that the D.E.s had been a drain on him physically and suggested this to his mother.

Mrs. R. wrote back, "I really want you to know the success of the release on Tim, my son. Aloa, it was *immediate*. The change in the child was like night to day. He is happier, doing better in school — and even told me he loved me! It's an entirely different child. There is no way for me to thank you enough."

She went on to say, "It bothers me that God would *allow* a child to be born with D.E.s inside him."

We must say here that many people, including myself, have wondered why this is permitted — and why discarnate entities are allowed to stay on the earth plane anyway? We are told that God has nothing to do with it. When He created man He gave him *free will* so when a person dies and leaves the physical body, he may stay on earth and be earthbound if he so chooses. If he does not realize he is dead, he will often stay around his home or place of work, wondering why he is not noticed!

Most D.E.s who realize their bodies are dead and that they are still very much alive, do everything in their power to take another body. That is why they stay around hospitals, waiting their chance to enter the body of a newborn baby. Most of the time the incoming soul is strong enough and enters first, blocking the entrance of a D.E. However, when there has been a long and painful birth, the body and aura are so weakened that one or more negative personalities can enter. We say "negative" because a positive, evolved entity would very seldom be earthbound and would never attach to another's body.

✧ ✧ ✧

Newborn Baby L. refused to take nourishment of any kind. She threw up constantly, and at the end of three days, was given up by the puzzled doctors who could find nothing physically wrong with her. The mother was still in the hospital and frantic, but her grandmother phoned to see if we could help.

When the analysis was done, it was found that several entities had entered the body at birth. The real self was trying to fight them off, and this was the cause of her trouble. After the release was completed, there was such a miraculous change that the doctors sent her home the next day! Her mother sent us a picture when L. was two years old – a darling child and healthy in every way.

✧ ✧ ✧

Little three-year old Sara had cried and screamed every night since she was born. She was very fearful and did not want her mother out of sight for a moment. She was referred to us and it was found that D.E.s had entered at birth.

After the release, her joyful parents reported that they had their first night of uninterrupted sleep since she was born. Her fear and anxiety were also gone and she is now a completely different child – happy and loving.

CHAPTER 6

Alcohol And Drugs

One of the most common ways for D.E.s to enter is through the use of alcohol or mind-expanding drugs. When we say "drugs", we mean anything that changes the brain or personality or that brings on a so-called "high ". We are referring to drugs like Marijuana, L.S.D., Cocaine, Morphine, or drugs that are sniffed, etc. Regardless of the harm they do to the physical body, especially the brain, they weaken and open the aura, often causing permanent "holes" in the aura. The D.E.s that come in are the lowest kind, those who have been drug addicts, murderers, and depraved in many ways. They often repeat their crimes through the body of the one possessed.

Bill wrote to us regarding the use of drugs to get into meditation. We replied:

"You are right that mind-expanding drug experiences can cause cracks or breaks in the aura, and almost without fail bring in entities. I do not believe in them *under any conditions* as no drug experience ever goes beyond the astral plane, and it is possible to have all the "good" drug-induced experiences during meditation when one allows himself to develop gradually, unfolding as the rose. As we discipline ourselves, learning to control thoughts and feelings, meditation experiences get better and better."

❖ ❖ ❖

Betty R. wrote, after her release: "I have smoked grass two different times, but again – I don't like what it does to me – *it takes away my high* – isn't that funny? If everyone that's into drugs could know this *high* – they wouldn't have to spend their money.

54

In the same letter, she comments, "I started taking diet pills again for awhile to 'take off weight', but I felt so bad, like I was backsliding – then   one day I threw away the bottle and said NO – it doesn't come from outside; it's all inside of me. God is the magic inside of me and nothing is as strong as that!

"Now looking back on this experience, I realize that I had to start taking diet pills to voluntarily throw them away – I AM STRONGER and they can never have an attraction for me ever again. Isn't that wonderful?"

We have nothing against diet pills in moderation, but they must be strictly under a doctor's supervision. We feel there are better ways to reduce. But any drug that makes one dependent or a slave to it should be avoided.

This is a heartbreaking case of Linda, who was deeply into a cult and later, drugs. Her mother wrote for help – and she was helped greatly with a miraculous change, but later became addicted worse than ever.

Mrs. A. (Linda's mother) wrote that her twenty-nine year old daughter had told her the year before that she had become a 'born again Christian', having joined a 'renegade group' designed to channel her every thought and movement in the name of Jesus. Since that time my daughter has fluctuated between severe depression and unnatural 'highs'. She lives by selling vitamins, collecting unemployment and working a few hours a day for a neighbor, and is living the life of a recluse. She has seen a psychiatrist who claims she has a 'chemical imbalance'.

"Then Linda had two incidents that terrified her. She saw what appeared to be footprints depressed into the coverlet of her bed. She screamed and left the apartment, and it was with great difficulty that she returned that night. When she got the courage to go to bed, she again saw footprint depressions on the bed and felt as though her entire body was taken over. She said she could not move, scream, open her eyes, or in any way control her body. Her mind was clear and she prayed until the entire room filled with light and the feeling finally left her. She is badly frightened... and I do feel she may be in danger of possession.

"My daughter is attractive, well educated and used to have a fairly good head on her shoulders. She has become frightened, unstable, unsure, unable to work, unable to love (she permits no man in her life), and unable to enjoy life in any way."

We found an infiltration of twenty-four extremely low D.E.s inside and outside the aura, causing emotional and physical problems. There was also a mind control (from the cult) giving mental problems, as well as three demons in her aura. After the release, inner stress went down one hundred and sixty-eight points to normal. Character came up six points to average, and there was a sixty-day restoration period indicated.

Linda's mother wrote three months later: "All that loving work you have devoted to my daughter, Linda, has been successful. She is FREE! She has left her secluded life and is back in the world again. She has gotten off unemployment insurance and is working four jobs simultaneously. I feel excess of any kind is potentially dangerous – but she says it doesn't bother her. She goes to her fourth job on Saturday. Linda is paying off all her debts and is determined to start afresh. I have no idea where she stands religiously – this is a subject I never approach – very definitely dangerous.

"From our conversations I pick up that she feels better about herself. She is so 'light' and I think has released the pain that brought her into the cult, and also the hostility she has carried towards me. I sent her the enclosure from the Unity and she accepted it with open arms. Did I mention that she went out on a date for the first time in almost a year?"

Nine months later, the sad news was received that Linda's life had again turned to dark. Her mother wrote that she felt the girl's life was in danger, "if not her life, certainly her mind".

"Linda phoned me at almost 5:00 A.M. yesterday,almost in hysterics", she said. "She had just wakened from a drugged sleep caused by taking something called 'Ludes'. She said she didn't know what kind of person she was becoming – didn't think she was fit to live. Then it was revealed that she is also using 'Speed'. So we have a young woman who is not functioning by her own mind at all – uppers during the day, downers at night – with only one goal, to get through the day. I begged her to function by herself but her answer was, 'I'm afraid. I can't stand the pain'."

We did not receive permission from our High Self to do another release for Linda until she was willing to stop the drugs, as the drugs would keep opening her up to more and worse entities.

❖ ❖ ❖

Mrs. K. wrote that she was deeply troubled by her husband's addiction to alcohol. She continued:

"Though he has seriously undermined a fine professional practice, lost most of his friends, and jeopardized his reputation through this addiction, he seems unable to help himself.

"Ever since a serious auto accident, drinking has caused him to be hostile, argumentative, and morose."

This was nearly fourteen years ago that the accident occurred. We found a deep infiltration of D.E.s inside and outside the aura, but especially inside the physical body. At the time, there were only eight D.E.s with him, but his psychic door was open, so they could come and go. Obviously, there had been many more before we measured.

After the release, inner stress went down one hundred and forty points to almost normal. Self evaluation, willpower, and determination were all below average and came up to average. He was given a restoration period of four months.

Mrs. K. wrote back about a week later to thank us for the work. She said, "Already I have noticed that he is more like his 'old' self than he has been for the past twelve plus years. I shall follow your suggestions, and will also include you and your work in my prayers."

We heard no more from her so assume he continued to improve.

❖ ❖ ❖

Pamela, now twenty-two, had been in and out of drugs all through her teens, with personality shifts and tensions. Alienation, rejection of all authority, and paranoia were aspects of the picture. At the time of release, she was recuperating from a severe case of jaundice and was very depressed. She was found to have thirty-one D.E.s inside and outside the aura and fifty-eight in her apartment. Her High Self was blocked and there were no spiritual guides with her. Inner stress was extremely high, and self evaluation, willpower, determination, and character were all well below average.

After the release, inner stress came down one hundred and sixty-six points and later dropped to average. Character, self evaluation and determination came up to average, but willpower was still somewhat below. However, a year later, this too had come up to average. Her High Self was in good contact and she had been given four spiritual guides.

Pamela's mother wrote to us two weeks later as follows:

"It is with joy and gratitude that I write to you as all that you said is coming about. My daughter has been with me this week and the qualities which I haven't seen in her for years are becoming manifest once more. The miraculous personality changes are clear evidence to me of the alterations brought about by drugs and the miracles wrought by prayer.

"My heart bounded with joy to hear her say, 'I feel as if I have been resurrected, my illness was a learning experience'. She is well aware that willpower and resisting others' influence in negative matters is where her work lies.

"Your news was manna to me and proof of powers and energies which I was not quite that certain of before. How D.E.s work and what openings we give them is now more apparent... Thank God for you and your work. That it is done in Christ's name is further assurance for me."

Gerald B.'s roommate wrote to us regarding a "desperate relationship that I am involved in... and he is slipping away or burning away because of a drug and drinking madness that a friend feels is caused by D.E.s. He is thirty-six years old and important in the artistic world, a director and creator. When he is not drinking, he is loving, giving, humane, passionate, understanding and compassionate, loving the world – and he expresses it in his work. When he starts to drink, he is the complete opposite and there is no way to reach him – he is someone else!"

We were told that Gerald had started taking drugs several years before and that was when his life fell apart. He added, "He feels that he is the cause of a suicide of a fellow actor in a theater he ran... The confusion around him is alarming."

Our analysis showed extremely low conscious and subconscious levels as well as no spiritual guides, and his High Self was completely blocked. There were thirty-nine D.E.s with him, including a partial possession inside the physical body, and the rest were inside and outside the aura causing emotional and physical problems. There were fifty-four D.E.s in the home. Character was extremely low as well as self-evaluation. We had to perform three releases before all the entities were finally taken by force by our helpers. His aura was so shattered it was necessary to do a recheck two weeks later when we found twelve D.E.s outside the aura only. This was quite a positive change.The last results we received were that Gerald was "not drinking at present" and too, was directing a play. "Very gifted", was the comment.

❖ ❖ ❖

Grace L. had a serious drinking problem, and although she had tried Alcoholics Anonymous for a while, a psychiatrist, and several "drying-out" hospitals, nothing seemed to help.

Our analysis for Grace showed that she had a very deep infiltration of thirty-two discarnates, including one in the physical body that was a partial possession. They were affecting her emotionally and physically and taking a great deal of energy. After the release, inner stress came down one hundred and thirty-seven points to nearly normal – there were two points to go during the restoration period of ninety days. Self-evaluation, willpower, and determination were all below average and came up to average, which was certainly to her credit.

Her friend wrote about six weeks later that "everyone noticed such a complete change. She has tried to stay away from alcohol, but I believe she has substituted drugs... But she is at last under the care of some institutional help."

We were glad to hear that Grace was receiving this extra help as it is often necessary in the case of long-standing alcoholism. But substituting drugs could only make matters worse. We did a recheck for Grace and found thirteen D.E.s inside and outside the aura, and they were released, along with more D.E.s in the home.

When we measured her again, she checked out clear. Her friend wrote, "Your clearing through Christ has helped create a miracle for Grace L. She is not even thinking of drinking and is pure joy to be around."

❖ ❖ ❖

Bill W. wrote that he had taken drugs, but didn't say what kind, and asked that we release any entities and cleanse his aura. He also said he did Transcendental Meditation.

In the analysis, we found there were thirty-four D.E.s with him, some inside the physical, as well as inside and outside the aura – and there were fifty-eight D.E.s in his home! Although his High Self was in contact, there were no spiritual guides with him. After the release, however, he was given seven guides, which indicated that his soul came in for definite spiritual growth. Inner stress came down one hundred and eighteen points, with five more to go during the restoration period. Self-evaluation had been below average and came up to average and his character came up seventeen points to "above" average.

We were gratified to receive the following letter:

"Ever since your wonderful work with me, I have been feeling lighter and more clear. My meditations are clearer now and I feel a strong energy and protection around me from the golden-white seal around my aura'... I truly appreciate your loving work and I love you very much for it and God bless you in the highest ways... Oh yes, I greatly enjoy my relationships with my spiritual guides and the Master. I talk to them and contact them often, expressing my love for them and my appreciation."

❖ ❖ ❖

Often it takes weeks or even months for an alcoholic to completely kick the habit after a release, but the following case was immediate. Mrs. P. sent us her husband's picture, saying: "He is an alcoholic and has created unbelievable problems for himself and those who have loved him, throughout his entire life... Situations in my life have become so unbearable that I don't feel I can go on much longer."

In our analysis for Mr. P., we found a very deep infiltration of twenty-six D.E.s – some inside the physical and others inside and outside the aura. And there was a supraphysical shell with him from a past life. His High Self was blocked and he had no spiritual guides. After the first release, we found there were three D.E.s that had refused to leave and these were taken away forcibly to the "fifth sun". Also, there had been thirty-one D.E.s in the home which were affecting other members of the family as well.

Mrs. P. wrote back, "I have to thank you, Aloa, I think you're wonderful. There has been a definite change in my husband. He has not (had a) drink for a week now – which is a tremendous improvement and he seems more self-confident and not quite so nervous." Mr. P. continued to improve and we were never asked to check him again.

The foregoing are just a few of the examples we have had where drug and alcohol abuse were caused by discarnate entities; in fact, a book could be written about only this one category! As prevalent as it is in our society, it is most gratifying to know it can be helped by releasing the negative entities causing it.

CHAPTER 7

High Level Negatives And The Left Hand Path

It has been found recently that negative forces can go as high in negative consciousness as can spiritual beings in their ascent in the Light. We are told there are at least twelve levels (probably more) of "Being" or consciousness growth and attainment and we are told that the Negatives can go just as far on the dark side as those in the Light. On the Right-Hand side or Positive High Levels, we find the great Masters, Archangels, and Spiritual Teachers of all time, many who are working to help mankind.

But on the left-hand side are the black magicians and very evil forces from the past who have "graduated" from the Lower Astral planes into the deeper levels of evil and satanic power. They do not attach to a human aura, but exert a powerful *Influence*. This can be felt as a draining of energy, confused thinking, and strange physical disturbances where a doctor can find nothing wrong! They work in different ways on different people so there are many symptoms. They are working extremely hard, especially on those of the Light, for they know their time is short.

We have had many, many of the above cases and every time it turns out to be Negative High Levels. Master Teachers have given us the correct method to remove and transmute their influence. There is a great Being outside of our Universe, the Lord Sarcasian, whom we are told to call to. He has the power to cut a person free from their influence. We ask for protection from his angel warriors in Scarlet and Gold. We also call to Lord Melchizidec and

Archangel Haniel, who work on levels closer to Earth. It *Works* and we thank God for this.

If there were no other sign of the last days of the old Piscean Age, the revival of witchcraft all over the world would be enough. This is especially true in England and America. We see witch covens on television where witches have been interviewed; also, information is given in the news and from those who have been affiliated with them. Of course, in Haiti and other Carribean islands and many third-world countries, witchcraft is still a way of life. They have always practiced these arts. For thousands of years witch doctors were the only means of healing and the use of magic was often used for good as well as evil. Their knowledge of herbs for medicines and even what we would call "psychology" has often been beneficent, if primitive.

For hundreds of years there have been tales of wicked witches, evil magicians, spells and enchantments that are usually associated with fairy tales. In the sophistication of modern civilization, many people are unaware that forms of magic still exist and are now being studied and used with renewed enthusiasm by modern-day witches and magicians.

We've all heard of the Haitian method of making a wax doll to represent an unwanted enemy and sticking pins in it to cause the person's death, as it reputedly does. Usually the person knows or expects that he is being worked on, and his own fear sets up a psychological reaction that destroys his will to live. His own belief that he will die often triggers the event!

Most witchcraft is used to influence someone else, to take away his free will and cause him to do the will of the one requesting the spell, making a hex to harm or even kill the person, or using strange brews or hypnotic chants to control. Often the victim is a relative of the one making the request, or an enemy.

All of the above are against God's law of love and freewill. We do not have the right to cause illness, take another life, or even control another person's life and therefore, it is WRONG. One doing this can only reap for himself untold sorrow and unhappiness. The Bible tells us, "For whatsoever a man soweth, that shall he also reap." Gal. 6:7.

"But", someone asks, "what about white magic which is used for good?" Witchcraft is called the "Old Religion" and indeed it is.

Its roots go back into very ancient times, even to the worship of the Goddess, when the leaders of religious organizations were female — priestesses. The use of magic was all they knew in order to bring about certain results. Today, witchcraft is a survival of this old religion which was a practice of using magical arts — potions, amulets, incantations, and later burning colored candles for the purpose of prophecy, causing someone to love another, heal sickness, destroy enemies, and often to interpret dreams.

At first, there was no distinction made between Black (malevolent) and White (benevolent) magic but later a distinction was made. Unfortunately, most witchcraft today is used for harmful purposes and promotes fear, not love. Satanism is another more violent form of the black arts which we will not go into. Animal and child abuse and torture as well as sacrifices are performed. For those interested, we recommend the book, *Breaking The Circle Of Satanic Ritual Abuse*, by Daniel Ryder.

Two thousand years ago, Jesus the Christ came to earth and brought the *new* religion of LOVE. He turned around all of the old concepts of serving one's self, of hating and destroying those one dislikes.

Jesus, said, "Love your enemies, bless them that curse you, do good to them that hate you, and pray for them which despitefully use you and persecute you." Matt. 5:44

Jesus knew the Law of Reversal, that by sending thoughts of good will, it would neutralize the evil they were sending and good would result. Jesus was, and *Is*, a Master of psychology and the power of thought. He taught the healing of sickness through the laying on of hands, a transfer of energy — God energy which is available to all who have faith. Faith is the catalyst that makes it work. It is this mighty God power, flowing through us, that is used to exorcise or release discarnate entities and their evil thoughtforms. The work is done in the Name of Jesus Christ because His power is as strong today as it was two thousand years ago, and He promised:

"In my name shall they cast out devils." Mark 16:17

The energy that witches and magicians use is a lower psychic energy which they can get from animals. Cats carry a great deal of psychic energy and that is why cats are often used in their rituals. There are also other forces in nature, invisible nature spirits, that are invoked and sometimes enslaved in order to do the bidding of the one making the call.

We wish to say here that any intentional misuse of God's laws can be construed as black magic! There are those who misuse prayer, having the effrontery to ask God to destroy their enemies or to bring about selfish requests that would bring harm or illness to others. Then there are leaders in some New Age groups who actually teach their followers to "decree" or chant harmful mantras such as, "annihilate, annihilate" against those who have left the group or are not in harmony with them. This writer knows of people who have died mysterious deaths or been killed in an accident after a group decreed in this way. *This is black magic!*

Belinda was a young lady who wrote to us for release. She had been a member of a cult and found out that the leader, "J", was using various methods of mind control and black magic to keep his members under his control. She left the group and wrote us for release from his power and any discarnate entities that she might have drawn. This was done, but she wrote later that "J" was doing everything he could against her – causing problems in her business and health, also that of her father. We did all we could to free her, but found that she had not entirely given up the negative teaching. A family member wrote that she, Belinda, was using black magic to control her and others.

We wrote Belinda as follows: "You asked me to check for spells on you and for D.E.s, which I did. But, Belinda, I know in the past *You* have used the black arts and put spells on people. You said you were all through with that after you left "J". I thought you could see how dangerous it is.

"I understand now that you are still doing these things to try to control people and get them to do what you want them to do and this evil energy is rebounding back to you and making you sick. Am I right? *We do not have the right to use force, mind control, incantations* or any other method to *Force* someone against their free will. This is against God's law and can only bring harm and sorrow to the one doing it. Those who take the path of the dark brotherhood will eventually lose their souls and have to go back to the beginning evolution and start all over again –working their way up through millions of years. That is, if they persist in their evil and do not turn to the Light.

"Belinda, if you want to have a joyous, fulfilling life, to love and be loved, then you must turn to God and ask His forgiveness and forgive yourself and follow the Light. When one works in the Light, he lets the God-power work through him, realizing he is only an instrument for good. "Not my will but Thine be done", as Jesus said. Those who work with the dark forces wield their own psychic power (or drain it from others) for their selfish purposes or to harm others. See the difference?

"May God in His love, guide you and touch your heart. He will help you if you ask Him, Belinda, and if you *Let* Him. Please do not write to me again for help unless you have completely put all this dark stuff behind you — you will only draw more entities to you."

Unfortunately, Belinda felt she could not cope with all the negativity "J" was heaping on her, and went back to his cult.

We deal with any type of black magic by first determining what kind is being used. We are aware of the following: mind control, hex, spell, curse, demons, and implant. These will be described in detail later. Then we call for the power of the Violet Transmuting Flame to dissolve and consume every vestige of the control, especially the "aka" cord, clear back to its source.

There are Angels of the Violet Flame who do this. The "aka" cord (aka from the ancient Hawaiian Kahuna term) is made of astral substance which connects the sender to the solar plexus of the one being controlled. (There are also good uses of the aka cord.)

After the violet flame has completed its work, the spot or spots on the body where the negativity was placed is cleansed and filled with a golden healing light and sealed with divine love.

✧ ✧ ✧

Vivian wrote to us that she was suffering from extreme nervousness, depression, and anxiety as well as many physical illnesses. She said that her aunt had practiced witchcraft on her since she was a baby, before the age of two and a half, using "extreme destructive hypnosis". She went on to say:

"She (the aunt) practiced witchcraft on me, programming me so as to trigger the physical and emotional illnesses she had set up in me through hypnosis, telepathically. I had also many discarnate entities around me which I could see. I have managed to free myself of them... but (my counselor) seems to feel that entities within my aura which are undetectable by me are the problem and that you can resolve it". She also felt the aunt had set up a negative forcefield around her to attract sadistic, destructive persons to her.

We will quote from the letter we wrote to her describing the findings:

"It has taken quite some time to complete the work and I am checking you almost daily. Your traumatic childhood experiences have left scars, and the astral and etheric bodies were badly damaged and there was some damage to the mental body. The healing may take some time.

"An analysis was done for you and the release completed on May 4. There was a very deep infiltration of discarnate entities inside the physical (a partial possession), entities inside and outside the aura, with an attachment on the astral and mental bodies. There was also a spell on you and an "implant" on the mental body as well as a powerful thoughtform on the subconscious. An implant is a controlling device, generally of astral substance, that is actually implanted by psychic means. Also, your "psychic door" at the base of the skull was open so the D.E.s could come and go. This has been closed and repaired, and a new doorkeeper (elemental) assigned.

"In rechecking on May 9, it was found that six D.E.s had refused to leave, so another release was completed and they were taken by the angels with their nets of golden light to the 'Fifth Sun'. On May 11 you checked out clear. All of the negativity has been removed, including spell, implant, thoughtforms, and the discarnates. However, there were also two supra-physical shells[1] from two different past lives.

"Remember, Vivian, everything that comes to us is for a purpose — there are no accidents — and karmic debts must be paid. I picked up three lives in which you were involved in black magic and it is possible, highly probable, that you performed similar practices on the one who is your aunt in this lifetime. It is no accident that she is your aunt! I get a life in England, one in South America, and one in Tibet in which you were involved in very destructive activities.

"You brought a great deal of strength with you to be able to free yourself of certain phobias and obsessions, as well as the D.E.s you could see. But the D.E.s inside you could not see, and they can also 'hide' in the aura. Inner stress was extremely high and came down one hundred ninety-two points to normal. Character was only two points below average and came up to average (another indication of inner strength). Self-evaluation, willpower and determination were all below average and came up to average. The restoration period should be about four months, depending on your work and attitudes.

"Now, on the positive side, here are some things you can do. First of all, *forgiveness*. It is important to forgive your aunt and all the destructive persons who were drawn to you. Remember, these could also have been ones you wronged in past lives – think about it – and most important, to *forgive yourself*. Here is a good affirmation, from Unity's Daily Word, to say over and over every day, with deep feeling – from your heart:

I forgive others and I forgive myself.
God forgives me and I am free.

Do this until you really feel cleansed and forgiven. I also detect fear in you, deep fear at the subconscious level. You must reprogram the subconscious." (We enclosed a sheet from Daily Word to help her in reprogramming.)

"Your High Self was in contact but you had no spiritual guides, or at least they were blocked. You now have five, which is a great blessing. Please keep in touch with me, Vivian, and let me know the results. With such deep scars, you may need more work as the healing progresses."

Vivian wrote back:... "I was very much impressed that you mentioned a number of things which I was already aware of although I did not mention them in my letter to you. I have also experienced a sense of release for which I am most grateful. The anxiety level has dropped considerably. I have looked in vain for years for someone who could understand and help me with this witchcraft problem, so I'm sure you can imagine how grateful I am to have your assistance."

We heard from Vivian over a period of several years for rechecks, clearing of a new residence, and so on. Her life became more and more positive and rewarding. Certain diets and physical therapy also alleviated her many physical symptoms.

When Clare wrote for help, we found she had eighteen D.E.s, five inside the physical body, and the rest inside and outside the aura. Her High Self was blocked and there seemed to be an attempted hex on her or some kind of black magic involved. It was found that one of the D.E.s inside the body had come from Haiti to the United States, where she later died. She had practiced voodoo and was trying to use this through Clare. It took three release sessions to finally complete the work.

A week after the clearing, Clare wrote this beautiful letter: "It finally seems that my wings have come out of my body, and my heart, my soul and my spirit are transcending the upward path to God and the heavens.

"I have noticed a change little by little every day in my life – it feels so good! How can one person tell you how grateful and thankful they are to you and God! My path is upward. God be with you."

Here is a case where the members of a whole family were under the influence of spells placed on them by a psychic healer from south of the border, whom they had been seeing. It is most likely she did this to keep them coming to her, insisting that all the unusual problems that kept coming up could be helped by her.

First, Jane, the daughter-in-law, wrote: "For about a year, and because of their own spiritual crisis, Peter's parents have been seeing a woman named Valencia. She is a "Santera" as I understand it, something like a psychic and a healer. At their insistence, Peter and I went to see her once and were impressed by her psychic ability. She wanted us to see her regularly, insisting that things were bad at work and that she could help us. We did not go back. She has sent us an afterbath water to apply each morning and lights candles to the Saints for us.

"Though I don't know why, I am ill-at-ease with Valencia and my in-law's faith in her... I believe that she is powerful in a way I don't understand. I have no reason to suspect that she wishes me any harm yet a caution and timidity make it impossible for me to proceed. I would appreciate any help you could offer. Sometimes I'm afraid that, instead of trying to help Peter and me, she would like to hurt us."

Then Peter's mother wrote asking us to clear their home and do some work for her, her husband, and a son and daughter living at home.

She said, "We have been seeing this lady, Valencia, and for a while it seemed like she was helping, yet I sense a change in her manner — I feel she is angry about something and this time I feel my family is threatened. I want you to know she has pictures of my daughter and two of my sons, as she said she works better with pictures.

The daughter at home, another married daughter, and a son not living at home also wrote us asking for a clearing.

Daughter Betty said, "I have been seeing a psychic by name of Valencia but things have gone from bad to worse. My personal life is just barely getting on its feet, my financial situation is disastrous. She also said she had been using the "bath water" for a few months but stopped using it as she had gotten hives. The doctor gave her a prescription but it did not help much.

All in all, there were eight people involved, all of whom had been seeing Valencia, with negative results. In checking each one of these people, we found spells as well as some D.E.s on most of them. Releases were done for all.

About a year later, Jane wrote, "Just a short thank-you for your special kindness and sensitivity in dealing with us and in helping Peter's family — a strange predicament to say the least.

"Peter and I are doing fine. The clouds seem to have cleared, and things look bright again... So far (our work) has been fairly well received. In fact, we landed our first assignment the day after you cleared us!"

❖ ❖ ❖

A woman we know who is psychically clairvoyant, had an interesting experience. Across the street from her lived a woman who was using witchcraft. Della had been in her home once and said she never wanted to enter it again, it was "creepy". There was a skull and crossbones dangling in her front window and many other strange, occult items in the room. Since Della was a spiritual teacher, this woman was not very friendly.

One morning when Della stepped on her front porch and started down the steps, a strange feeling stopped her. She felt that some kind of barrier was in front of her. When she looked with her inner eye, sure enough, there was an object like a bench across the walk and Della almost walked right into it. This could have caused a bad fall and accompanying problems. Here is a good example of a hex.

✧ ✧ ✧

The following surprising case may be more common than we suspect. Unfortunately, jealousy and desire for power can affect spiritual leaders and ministers as well as laymen.

Rev. Abigail Z. was the founder of a thriving little church in the northwest and had been the pastor since its beginning. She was also, it appears, well versed in occult practices as well. She began putting spells on anyone in the church whom she felt threatened her, and this applied to three especially – Arthur, the president of the church board; Marie, a musician; and Fletcher H., one of the pianists. It was Fletcher who wrote to us, asking for help.

One Sunday morning, he went to the piano to play for the morning service and noticed that his hands were becoming paralyzed! He exerted all of his power to press down the keys and when he did, to his horror, he played the wrong notes. He felt completely taken over by some force – and this lasted until the service was over. When he arrived at home, he had to go to bed, his energy was so drained. Marie, who played a prelude of classical music before the service, told him later that she had had the same trouble – her fingers simply wouldn't work right.

Later in the week, he felt impressed to speak to Arthur about it. Arthur was relieved because he had felt the same force grip his vocal cords when he was at the pulpit and he could barely speak.

Fletcher phoned us and we worked in our service group, asking that Abigail's power for evil be dissolved and that the spells on these three be broken and consumed back to their source. We also sent love to Abigail and asked that she be awakened to the evil she was doing.

We asked for her highest good and greatest potential. Fletcher wrote to thank us but also asked that we continue the work and that Rev. Abigail had left on a month's vacation. This was good news and we prayed that during that month changes would take place. However, he added that two Sundays ago she had projected into the service and usurped energy from all those on the program.

71

He said, "Marie and I were affected least because she didn't know we were going to be on the program. We have run tests on this and know for a fact that this is happening.

"Well, this last Sunday I arrived early... and was going to set the tone for the service but when I began to work, I was impressed that someone had put a spell on the chapel and house. Never having been exposed to spells and the dismissing of them, I had no experience in dissolving them. But I was filled with the Holy Spirit and broke into prayer... and the Very God of Very Gods, the Holy Spirit descended on that chapel like a dove. The dove of peace was there and I started claiming this little center for God. I started denying that Abigail P. had any ownership in it and started affirming that we were preparing the way for the Christ. 'Sanctus, sanctus, sanctus' rang out of my voice... What a holy sanctuary it was and what a wonderful Christ-filled service we had (and continue to have, using this same technique)."

Fletcher asked that we pray for Arthur, the president of the Board. "He is doing his best to keep everything running smoothly but he's really in the firing line of Abigail since he works with her closely. He says he is really weakened when he stands at the pulpit to speak. This is when she does her work."

We were also told that Abigail did not like the classical music Marie played for the prelude ("that longhaired stuff" she called it) so she put her in a psychic paralysis which would completely usurp any inspiration — Marie said her hands would turn into clay. Fletcher experienced this too when he would play or accompany someone.

He went on to say, "Anything that threatens her, she eliminates — especially the wives of the men who start coming to church. She insults them in one way or another until they stop coming". (Fletcher had told us previously that although Abigail was married, she had a special liking for men, but not their wives.) He continued, "She takes one's self-respect, and you can bet that if a situation can be handled gently and beautifully with soft words, she will handle it by bawling someone out in front of the whole church. I am giving you a small sketch of how things have gone."

We continued to work in the group, but Abigail returned at the end of the month and Fletcher reported that Arthur was having a particularly bad time. At the Christmas program, he was platform chairman and doing all the announcing. He said he was put into a paralysis as he stood at the podium and all evening felt as weak as water and totally cut off. (Fletcher was at home in bed because of her psychic attack for it appeared that she was not going to have him participate in her Christmas program!)

As we continued to work, there were good times and bad times at the church. We had given Fletcher several methods of protection to use for himself and the church and he reported that one Sunday morning while Arthur was giving the announcements, she suddenly jumped up, stepped down from the platform and ran out of the church and did not return! Fletcher found out later that she had gone home to bed with a splitting headache.

We had to ask Fletcher not to keep repeating over and over what Abigail was doing, "As in this way you are giving her power, you are strengthening the energy cord (aka cord) between you. We worked so hard to break it, but when you think or write about these attacks, it is re-energizing the whole thing."

We told him he must break it by visualizing a blue-white sword from Archangel Michael and cut himself free. "If any of you begin to feel her at work in church, immediately think, 'You have no power. God is my power', and give a cut with that blue sword, like a Karate cut – right in front of you, even if you are at the piano or in the pulpit. It will be short and quick and should not be noticed."

After having worked several months for Abigail, who showed no signs of responding, we felt directed to just place her in God's hands and discontinue all work. In the meantime, Fletcher had only been attending church when he was sure she would not be there and finally left the church permanently. He said he felt he had learned the lessons he had been sent there to learn and the experiences were necessary for his growth and future service.However, Fletcher later sent an update: "The little church has fallen completely under Abigail's black magic spell, for after visiting while she was out of town, the negative vibrations were so noticeable. She manages to mesmerize and subliminally hypnotize the members of the board for not only does she perform malpractice work to eliminate, but she also works on people's minds, implanting subliminal thoughts on how great and wonderful she is. The point is that if she had expended all of that energy used to do the black magic work (and it takes a tremendous amount) toward working in the Light, how blessed she would be and how blessed others would be."

✧ ✧ ✧

According to our understanding, an "implant" is a type of control device, usually made of astral substance and implanted in the head area of the mental body or the astral body. This is usually done from the astral realm by a group of former black magicians who work with the interplanetary dark forces. They choose those whom they feel they can best use and who can be easily penetrated and used. Those who are strong can also be attacked in moments of weakness, illness, or when unprotected.

An implant can also be made from the earth level through hypnosis. Never, never allow anyone to hypnotize you unless you are positive of their credentials and have fully checked them out with those who have benefitted from them. We do not recommend hypnosis, regardless, as it can be dangerous to the higher mental body. It often breaks the etheric web between the etheric and astral bodies.

In Margie's case, the implant manifested as a voice. After the release, she reported that she was much better, could think clearly, but still had the voice. There had also been a few D.E.s inside and outside the aura and in the home, which had all been cleared.

We had picked up the strong feeling that a woman in her city was responsible for the implant. She knew who Margie was but Margie didn't know her. The woman was using her "powers" for fun and kicks. The"aka" cord between the two was dissolved as well as the woman's power over Margie. A tape was also made for Margie to play over and over to rehabilitate the subconscious and remove the habit patterns, as explained under "Voices".

Three months after the release, when restoration should have been complete, Margie reported she still heard voices but she thought some were "good." This was not true as they often start out sounding very benevolent until the person is hooked, then they become mean and destructive. In checking again, we found there were five D.E.s involved, some on the astral plane and some earthbound. However, we also discovered that Margie's "psychic hearing" was open — that the web between the astral and etheric bodies was very thin and damaged. This Margie confirmed — she said she had felt it. We worked to repair this web and close off the psychic hearing.

Margie phoned three days later that she was very much better — that there was no sound in her ear and the voices were gone! She also added that on the very day we were working, she had seen a long flash of blue-white light and thought it "was from Aloa".

She also wrote later, "Several months ago, I spoke with a woman who is very clear-sighted. She wondered why I was surrounded by a protective light — I believe blue or white. I told her I had had trouble and had been cleared. She said that explained it — that the work done was excellent and had left me sealed. Again, thank you!"

◇   ◇   ◇

We were sent a very detailed account of a most unusual experience. Miranda is a light worker and counselor who has had several psychic attacks, but this was the most extreme. She says she remembers nothing of what happened — not even the arrival of the paramedics and ambulance ride to the hospital! Her husband told her what had happened and she related the following story:

"On a Sunday night, I was very tired and went to bed early. And because I was so tired, I may have forgotten to put myself in protection. John was watching television and said he heard some strange noises and found me in the front hall, rather disoriented and concerned because I 'couldn't find him'. He got me back to bed and calmed me down, but a short while later he heard a piercing scream from my room. He rushed in and I was crying and babbling in a strange language and my body was trembling and shaking. He held me in his arms and got me quieted down and apparently asleep. Then he decided to get ready for bed.

"Again came the same piercing scream and he rushed in to find me sobbing and mumbling. This time my body became rigid and the trembling didn't stop, so he called the emergency number and the paramedics came and took me to the hospital. There had been a slight bit of foam in the corner of my mouth and they called it a kind of seizure. I was given an intravenous solution to balance the body chemicals as they felt the potassium — sodium was out of balance. By Monday breathing had become impaired and they thought I might have regurgitated a little and some of the stomach fluid got into the lungs. Later they placed me in intensive care when I suddenly stopped breathing and they hurriedly connected me to a breathing machine with oxygen, and other equipment. I had come down with pneumonia! I have no memory of the next six days, only when they put the tube down my esophagus and I remember a loud voice saying sharply, '*breathe, breathe*'.

With all my might I took a breath.

"A week later I started coming back to consciousness and I remember the nurse saying, 'Your John is here with you'. I learned later they had given me morphine to keep me quiet.

"After I came home and started to recuperate, I felt rather strange — not like myself. I felt 'pulled apart' as if part of me were somewhere else. I found it very hard to concentrate, hard to think while talking, and my mind would sometimes just go blank. We asked Aloa to check me out and there were a few D.E.s outside the aura which were released. But I was no better.

"Ten months later, I had another attack during the night, but not as severe. I remember the paramedics coming and the ambulance ride to the hospital. They sent me home the next day with the admonition to see a certain brain specialist for an E.E.G. test. They had given me a CAT scan at the hospital but it showed nothing. After the E.E.G. test, the doctor told us all he could find was a slight 'short circuit' in the left temple area and put me on a mild dosage of Dilantin.

"About sixteen months later, a very spiritual lady with inner sight came from another city to visit. Before she left, she asked if I would like to have a reading, which I was grateful to accept. Then she announced that there was something in my left temple that had been implanted by an astral group of the dark forces! So I told her about the two seizures I had had which the doctors had labeled 'epilepsy'. She said, 'You don't have epilepsy — this is a very deep psychic implant'."

Miranda asked to have a release done right away and felt much better afterwards, but we realized it would take several sessions to remove it all. The next day some more work was done, and the third day, our whole Light Group worked to remove it, dissolve and consume it and break the "aka" cord connecting to the astral group. It took three days to build up the energy and it was powerful. The angels of the Violet Flame and Archangel Michael's angels removed every vestige of it.

Immediately, Miranda felt a great freedom and a feeling of wholeness. She said, "For the first time in two years I really felt like myself – I felt all together. I had had pains in the left temple – sharp twinges that would come and go or an ache in that area – not continually, but often. I have had none of that since the release, and it is now six months. I feel alert when I talk to people and that 'spaced-out' feeling is gone. How very, very grateful I am and how I thank all of you and the angelic beings."

She added, 'Naturally, I did not tell the doctor, but I have cut down on the Dilantin with no ill effects and will soon discontinue completely."

❖ ❖ ❖

We feel it would be well here to include some – information on psychotronic implants and subsequent injuries, as published by Dr. Andrew Michrowski in his monograph, P.A.C.E.

He says a USSR scientist, Litisitsyn, reported that the "Soviet scientists have developed and fitted a theory to actual brain wave measurements, and could insert material on electromagnetic carriers directly into the brain and could control whether or not the process stimulated conscious awareness of the individual".

"The monitoring of time coherent and phase-locked psychoactive modulations suggests strongly the following: The psychoactive modulation effectively locks in the multiple carrier frequencies (say 11-23). On these locked-in multichannels, brain-coded information is inserted, feeding it directly into the captured target brains. Potentially, almost anything could be inserted into the target brain/mind systems, and such insertions would be processed by the biosystems as internally generated data/effects. Words, phrases, images, sensations and emotions could be directly inserted and experienced in the biological targets as internal states, moods, emotions, thoughts, and ideas.

"While the state of the art of the USSR techniques undoubtedly poses some practical limits, a mind control and behavior-control weapon of enormous and frightening possibilities, capable of directly affecting huge populations anywhere in the planet now appears to be in the hands of the USSR. Furthermore, the weapon appears to be engaged in actual calibration and alignment against... populations on the North American continent."

We have not had any experience with the above and do not wish to frighten people. But we must be *aware* and *know* that God's power can and will protect us if we ask and consciously use His shield of White Christ Light around us. Do read the 91st Psalm.

If you wish any more information on the above, you may write to:

Dr. Andrew Michrowski
c/o P.A.C.E
100 Bronson – Suite 1001
Ottawa, K1R – 6G8
Canada

CHAPTER 8

Voices And Suicide

Many, many people have the problem of "hearing a voice" in their heads. This is usually not an audible voice (although sometimes it is) but a strong, persistent, intelligible but inaudible sound inside the head. Often the voice will begin by saying very fine, complimentary things in order to get the victim's attention. Many think they are hearing the "voice of God" or of some saint or master. Then when the victim is "hooked", the voice will begin to say stupid, silly, or obscene phrases, often urging the person to commit suicide or murder. Of course, this is always the work of a very vile discarnate entity.

Brenda wrote us from a sanitarium where she had been staying for several months, and said she was on the verge of suicide. This urge to commit suicide was caused by an inaudible voice in her head that went on incessantly, telling her to kill herself. This continued on and on until she thought she was losing her mind and was ready to end it all when she wrote us. She also said she had been quite ill for several years, but about two and a half years previously had gradually gone into a deep fear about anything and everything, especially her health. These were years of depression in which she took a leave of absence from her job. She had already been in psychotherapy, but the fear seemed to deepen further, always with the voices in the background urging her to kill herself.

In early July, Brenda had gone to bed one night, feeling as usual toward her husband of fourteen months, but awoke the next morning with such antagonism toward him that she frequently gagged when he spoke to her and this lasted for fifteen horrifying months!

She also had feelings of being someone "different" and at times had spells of shaking inside and out. Once in a while she would feel like her former "stable" self, but gradually grew pale and transparent-looking.

She said, "This traumatic sequence of reactions really drove me to the edge of despair as it made me terribly depressed and afraid night and day that I would be driven to suicide."

We found that Brenda's High Self was blocked and that there was a possession inside the physical body. There were many D.E.s inside and outside the aura as well, affecting her both emotionally and physically. There were also many D.E.s in her home, which was also cleared.

After the release was completed, she wrote a glowing letter: "Your work has been a tremendous help and my husband could tell right away that there was a difference in me."

After she received our letter giving the time of release, Brenda said that she had mentioned to her husband that she felt the lift of a burden about that specific time and she had wondered if we had been working for her. Also, she found the voices had disappeared! However, for the next two days she had experienced some very difficult hours of total body aching, which of course, was part of the body reaction.

She added, "The rest of the week until today has seemed as if I'd had emotional surgery."

Brenda has kept in touch with us over the years and referred many people. She has been choir director in her church and has written some exquisite music for choir and organ. She and her husband are having a joyous and fulfilling life.

❖ ❖ ❖

We worked with Joan for over a year because of disturbing voices and other problems. It seemed every time she wrote she would describe a condition she had forgotten to mention before. When she first wrote, she had attended a "Regression" class and then mind control classes. The regression took her supposedly to a past life in a concentration camp in Nazi Germany.

Our analysis showed D.E.s inside and outside the Aura, and

a complete possession in the physical body, which were affecting her emotionally and physically. We asked her to do nothing of a psychic nature for at least four months. Also, we found that when she had been regressed, it had torn open her "psychic web" between the etheric and astral bodies.

After the release, she wrote that she felt fine but still had "distant voices that come and go in intensity". We felt this was residue — a habit pattern, and that she must tune them out. However, she wrote that her husband had insisted she see a doctor who had put her in the hospital for three days. There was no improvement. She also had been to a hypnotist, and this opened her up to more D.E.s, so another release was done. Hypnotism may not harm everyone, but Joan's aura was so damaged and proper protection had not been used.

Later she wrote that she still had "echoes" and also mentioned popping noises in her head which began soon after the mind control classes. We found a few more D.E.s outside the aura — they were going in and out as the psychic door was open by that time. This was closed and a new doorkeeper assigned.

Then she wrote us, casually mentioning that she was a very heavy smoker — two packs a day, and that her body had as much nicotine as a body can stand! No wonder she had the whirling feeling she had described, and also more holes in her aura. Nicotine also affects the circulation and brain responses. There were more D.E.s with her and another release was performed.

Finally, seventeen months after the work began, she wrote: "This is just a short note to tell you I am fine. It was a long hard journey, but I'm out of the pit. The road stretches before me straight and true. I don't know where I'm going, but God does and that's enough for me... The voices are still with me, but have changed as I grow stronger and surer. I was told several months ago to continue to meditate and pray, something you told me from the beginning... It has been a fight every step of the way, but well worth it. I would never have emerged from the cocoon without the struggle."

There were many others also praying and helping Joan, both in the church and in metaphysics. But she wrote so lovingly of our work: "I have so much to tell you but the most important is that the love you sent was the first pure love I felt. Without you I would not be sitting here writing. You are stronger than any other who does the type of work you do. This I know, because I have been told. I feel you with me much of the time. I send you love and energy when I meditate, for you need the prayers too. (Indeed we do!) When I told one of the deacons of the church about you and that I would not be here without what you did, he said he knew and believed".

✧ ✧ ✧

A very unusual case was that of Jennie who was on the verge of suicide when she contacted us. She complained of a force that made her do "idiotic, moronic" things all day, and make costly mistakes in her work. Also, she was bothered by voices.

We found a partial possession with her and other D.E.s inside and outside the aura. Some were so determined to stay that it took three sessions to clear her. She felt much better but wrote two weeks later that the "voices" were back. We found that the D.E. was indeed gone but her subconscious was programmed to listen for voices and was replaying the old "record".

A cassette tape was made for Jennie to play over and over to clear the subconscious mind of the old habit pattern.

Jennie was better for a month, then phoned that a deceased man she had known, G.W., was harassing her from "the other side." We checked and found it was not G.W. but a Luciferian station or power center in the astral level which was partly run by robots. They were broadcasting (like psychotronics) and people who had weak or damaged auras or were psychically tuned in to their frequency, would pick up the harassment.

We have a service group that convenes once a week, so we worked on this as a group. Through angelic help, a huge pyramid of white light was established over the entire center (invisible to them) so they could not contact anyone on the earth plane. Jennie was cut free and the astral tie-in to them was dissolved and consumed in the Violet Flame.

Jennie got along pretty well for the next three months, and then began having trouble again. She sent us a copy of her astrological chart. Usually D.E. attachments do not show up on a chart unless there is a karmic reason; however, we are not astrologers, but certain aspects formed to Neptune in the third house. Her Sun squared Pluto but Uranus trine Pluto helped to offset it. Sun square Pluto also tends to show a possession we are told. In analysis, her astrologer said that she was subject to invasion by D.E.s and that she carried negative power – a strong will that she brought with her and any emotional disturbance could open her up.

She added, "There is hope if she is willing to sacrifice. She has gone through some very hard lives. She must stay away from environmental influences like bars, discos, etc. In the immediate past life she was involved with negative psychism – it showed in her eyes and face. However, every aspect is separating and moving out. She has tremendously powerful will and can turn it around and use it to overcome. Mercury is moving out of the opposition to Uranus and Mars is moving away from Neptune."

Jennie worked very hard on herself but continued to have trouble from time to time. We had recommended a Biometric Analysis and the Bach Flower Remedies from a very fine coworker in California. Jennie accepted this, but a month later asked us to recheck. There were no D.E.s attached but we found a group of five astral entities that were attacking her in the solar plexus (which she could feel). They went willingly into the light.

The next month she asked for another recheck. We found a "thoughtform" attached on the astral body in the solar plexus area. This had been blocking the effect of the Bach Flower Remedies. The thoughtform was dissolved and Jennie was told that she must use love and forgiveness to this group of thirteen that had placed it on her, as she had worked with them in the past. They were taken by the angels to the "Fifth Sun".

It was eight months before another recheck was requested and we found eleven D.E.s inside and outside the aura. They were removed. By this time Jennie was much better and most of her symptoms had disappeared. She had been working very hard, with the help of others, to strengthen her weak aura, to change her thoughts and feelings, and to raise her consciousness to a higher level.

However, the next year she was troubled again with a voice that was very persistent. Our work did not seem to help until we discovered that an "instrument" or recording device had been implanted in her astral body and the voice was constantly played over and over to harass her. These lower astral forms simply would not give up — she had worked with some of the various groups in several lifetimes and had even been a leader.

This device was removed and dissolved and the spot sealed with light. Jennie continued to work in the light with her tremendous willpower.

It is now over three years later. The last I heard from Jennie, she was free from D.E. influence, including voices and psychic attacks. Her intense work with forgiving others and herself for her negative work in the past and replacing it with love really paid off. She learned to love herself as well as others. Her aura was healed and strengthened and her whole life improved in so many ways as she yielded herself to God's Divine Plan for her life.

✧ ✧ ✧

Betty was a young woman whose mother wrote to us for help. She was very disturbed, neglecting her family, and unable to control her outbursts of temper.

Her mother wrote that shortly before writing us, Betty had slashed her wrists. She did not hurt herself badly and it was felt that this was rather a plea for help.

A few days after the release, her mother wrote, "She seems to be almost one hundred percent better! I feel she is at least trying. She brought her children out last evening for Christmas Eve and all went very well."

✧ ✧ ✧

Barbara was a model and her mother wrote that she was in desperate need of help as she was on the verge of suicide. She had been the victim of a very bad marriage and had just received a divorce, yet was very disturbed.

Our analysis showed that there were thirteen very destructive D.E.s with her, one inside the physical body (a partial possession) and the rest inside and outside the aura, as well as some demons. The negative vibrations were affecting her emotionally and physically, as well as mentally.

A release was done for Barbara, but the next day when we rechecked, there were four left that had refused to leave. They were removed forcibly by the In-God-We-Trust angels and then her measurements showed a remarkable change even though there was a ninety-day restoration period indicated.

A month later, her mother wrote,"Upon opening your letter, I felt the love of God released with it, and I knew all was well. Barbara has improved daily and is almost the same person we once knew. She says it is so wonderful to live without thinking of suicide, and she laughs again. She prays again. Thank you for using your gift for good."

At the end of two months we were asked to check her again and she was found to be still clear and in good balance.

It is pretty well agreed upon in most religious circles that there are dark forces about, be they called devils, demons, ghosts, discarnate entities or Satan and Lucifer. Many clergymen believe Satan and Lucifer to be one and the same, but we feel they are not. At this time (and we are open to change) we believe Satan to be a composite force of evil, created by the dark thoughts and deeds of mankind since man first stepped on earth. Through aeons of time it has acquired consciousness, power, and a type of mental ability which is fed and expanded by man's evil thinking. There are many discarnate entities as well as embodied individuals who serve and worship this evil force, thereby strengthening and enhancing its power.

Lucifer, on the other hand, was a Son of God who, with the Christ, was with Him before the creation of our star system. Lucifer was given rulership over a beautiful planet located in our solar system between what we call Mars and Jupiter, and in some ancient writings was called Maldek. Lucifer, in Hebrew, means "light bearer" or "morning star", and his position as ruler of this exquisite planet was one of great honor.

Eventually, desire for more honor and power began to gnaw at him and he gradually felt that he could set himself up even above God, the Supreme Source. It is said that he and his cohorts had discovered the use of atomic fission and even the hydrogen bomb. Apparently he felt that by obtaining the power of a hydrogen explosion, if all went well, he could have the great creative power of God.

But all did not go well and the Luciferians blew up their planet, completely destroying it, and leaving only a belt of asteroids in that space, it is surmised. Most of the population was taken to safety in another solar system before the destruction, but

Lucifer and his cohorts were brought to the earth. The Bible alludes to this in Isaiah 14:12-14: "How art thou fallen from heaven, O Lucifer, son of the morning!... For thou has said in thine heart, I will ascend into heaven, I will exalt my throne above the stars of God... I will ascend above the heights of the clouds: I will be like the most high."

And so it seems Lucifer and his hosts are still on earth tempting mankind and using his energy for their own purposes.

The story of Sara Lin and her redemption from the powers of Lucifer is most unusual. Even if you do not believe that you have lived previous lives on earth (reincarnation), please read this with an open mind.

When Sara Lin wrote to us for help early in 1979, she was constantly being attacked by a group of very negative forces who called themselves names like "Daddy", Lucifer, and "A". In our studies, we have found that most of the Luciferians incarnated into human bodies from time to time, and throughout the ages have attempted to wield their power over mankind, probably as some of the more ruthless leaders in our history. They can be recognized by their greed for personal power and absolute control.

On the lower astral levels of the inner-plane worlds they function as groups that harass and attack weak souls on earth, especially any who have worked with them and are trying to break free. We doubt very much that Sara Lin is a Luciferian, but she was a follower for several lifetimes, possibly having been coerced into joining the group in the beginning.

Since these forces were not actually attached to her but were attacking from the outside, they could not be exorcised, although she also had D.E.s that were attached. But we called mightily on the Powers of Light, the Christ forces, to intervene and cut Sara Lin free from the evil control and take away their power.

The first time we did an analysis for Sara Lin, we did not realize the extent of her problems. At that time she told us it was a long-standing problem and that entities of a "brutish nature seem to use a shell or astral blanket over the head to get me, particularly in the middle of the back, the third eye, and navel chakra". She added that she had tried everything and on occasion, had been able to shut them out but "they pick or hammer their way back in... It seems when I meditate or am attuned spiritually, they enter along the top of the head (along silver cord)."

We found sixteen negative D.E.s inside and outside the aura, but oddly no possession. There were, however, demons with her as well as entities in the home. A complete clearing was done. At this time, we were under the impression that most of these evil forces were the D.E.s attached to her. We were not aware that they were astral entities and demons of the dark forces. However, her psychic door was open so they could come and go at will and this was closed and sealed.

Sara Lin, however, did feel she had been helped to a degree. "Since writing to you", she wrote, "have felt and known I have help consciously – a marvelous feeling. Know I've had help before but am now conscious of it. I am feeling more centered and feel this (problem) will come to an end.... Was glad to know of the white tube of light... It makes them angry... am still experiencing a lot of harassment and there is a constant contest continuing through sleep and every waking moment... I see these black things on the floor, black (forms), and I also see lights.

"After thirteen years", she continued, "I don't hesitate to try to destroy them. They try to occupy my third eye. They still talk about their 'Daddy' and use words of power, and say they want my name... I have a long background in metaphysics with Science of Mind as my foundation. I also play cassettes of enlightened people and burn candles to keep vibrations up. Aloa, my goals since the early sixties have been the spiritual path and I am so thrilled to hear I have six spiritual guides. When free of these 'uglies' I can attune myself to 'Good' – to the wonderful God vibration."

More work was done for Sara Lin and we found rather startling information. We wrote, "You have been clear the last two times I checked you, including today. All these forces that are attacking you in the various spots you mention, I believe, are demons – possibly that you yourself created in past lives, and they have been drawn to you in this one. This includes the one called Z—, I don't want to use his name and give it energy. A demon is an energized thoughtform creation, not a discarnate entity. Some people are highly developed in thoughtform creation and can empower these forms with subtle energy so they materialize. The ancient Tibetans were masters at this.

"Now, when you first begin to feel these forces, surround

yourself in the Christ Light and put all fear in His hands. Then say with strength and feeling, even bellow it with great force:

'I created you and I now dissolve you'.

Say it three times and if it does not disappear, it is an entity rather than a demon. But you can still command it to *be gone* and not return."

We also gave her more instruction on protecting herself:

"Now, you must get your sleep without fear of attack. When you get in bed, put the tube of white light around you and a 'platform' of golden light under the bed, with a cross of blue flame over the top of your head and on the solar plexus. Say the twenty-third psalm and ask Jesus Christ to send you special angels of protection to stand guard over all your bodies, physical and subtle. Then just let go all anxiety and drop off to sleep like a child in its mother's arms."

The first year seemed to be one of gradual improvement, although the attacks continued. Sara Lin reported that right after she had mailed a letter to us, she felt a sense of relief. There was still interference with any spiritual study but on a more subtle level. Attacks on her body were continuing in the third eye area (forehead) and she added, "They try to hide from those who can perceive them".

We had fourteen sessions for Sara Lin the first year, and during that time there were sometimes two or three D.E.s outside the aura, which was still not completely healed. However, entities were not the problem, it was far more deepseated.

Work was continued with Sara Lin during the second year when she wrote without mentioning a psychic attack and we assumed she was free. But this was without foundation, for she replied:

"I did not discuss attacks because I am never without some form of dark force trying to influence me. I did rid myself of a lot of things of my origin, frustrations etc., but there is one, when challenged, who says his name is 'A'... and another, when challenged, says he is Lucifer, and they continually plague me. Those that work for the one called 'Daddy' are here also but I do not know what they are — whether thoughtforms I had conjured up from a past life or what.

"But", she continued, "on the positive side, severe attacks

have been fewer. Health is improving gradually and I have been able to feel more of an attunement with Christ. My attitude is better and my desire to live, stronger... Thank you again, Aloa, your letters are always a ray of hope and sunshine much needed."

We continued to work with Sara Lin from time to time, often asking others to help in the work or doing it in our light group.

Then she wrote, "I felt cleared on Sunday – felt so wonderful not to have anything pressing in on me or occupying my spine. Most of the time I am smothered and when free, get so much light and energy. Then on Monday, felt a pressure on my back between the shoulder blades, a cutting off of my light, and by evening they had broken through. They use a shell or another entity to get to me... no matter how hard I try, what mantra I say or light I use, I cannot seem to prevent them."

About this time, Sara Lin phoned two days in a row and we were impressed to work for three days, praying that their power be dissolved and consumed and that all ties to Sara Lin be broken. She seemed to be better and we did not hear for three months. Then a phone call that she was being harassed again. Another session was held for her, and she wrote the following note:

"It was very good talking to you. I did receive some help this morning but again, they were able to break in. I have been asking that their minds be filled with light. *They keep telling me to return to sorcery* but there is one that says he intends to kill me... They rob me of energy through the back of the neck, my sides, and the base of the spine... Again, when I awoke this morning, it was with the presence and speech of a Lucifer. It seems they all work together. I do not understand the *determination* of these entities but they want to keep me from my path. Sometimes when the fight is very strong, one will say, 'Why don't you fall, dammit?'... they are really fighting to take over my body movements. I drop things, and they fight for control of my car."

Shortly after this, we called in two spiritually oriented friends, one, an Indian woman who was clairvoyant. We held a service from eleven to midnight, calling on the Christ forces and Archangel Michael, and Hazel used some of her Indian prayers of banishment. Hazel said that Sara Lin was "wide open" – not protected, and that her protective words were not from the heart, also that the retribution she was paying was from a combination of lifetimes. (We were well aware of this!) She added that we could keep her clear for one week and then she must build her own protection.

Hazel saw three lives that were contributing in part to this one – a gypsy life where she worked with these dark forces, an American Indian life when she started to change, and a Mexican life about the time of the conquistadors when she was back with the dark forces.

In spite of all the spiritual yearning and effort, it was felt that Sara Lin was allowing human flesh to rule her life, not the spiritual. She was told to start a cleansing, beginning with the root chakra and on up, cleansing the seven chakras that were clogged with residue, heaviest around the heart. We had also suggested earlier that Sara Lin send love to these forces – the powers of darkness cannot stand *love*.

She replied that it did no good, adding, "I do not believe that love is the answer. Neither love nor hate, for they (or most) are totally beyond redemption, their minds having become entirely satanic until they are no longer themselves, but automatons of dark forces... These are sorcerers who need energy and bodies for their black work. When I contest them, they scream they need my energy. They use different terms but they are the same old ones, using the old female to reach me and shove ugly black stuff through my chest area. They enter at will. I contest them, many times all night, and getting ready to go to work, with no rest. My hearing (inner) has increased and one tells me they are of the Black Lodge. They also tell me that one is 'Rasputin'."

We realized by this time that it was Sara Lin herself who had to banish and completely overcome these forces, but we continued to help. She asked to come to see us in person just before Christmas of 1981. We felt we should do this and invited her to stay for two days.

One might have expected a rather nervous person, highly emotional and even mentally unstable considering all the years of psychic attacks Sara Lin had been subjected to. But we met a beautiful lady, surprisingly stable emotionally, mentally alert, and spiritually attuned. She was a member of a small church and by this time was teaching classes and doing some counseling.

We found she had had a very traumatic and disruptive

childhood and left home at the age of sixteen. She had a bad marriage which ended in divorce and was trying to support herself and son. Then another marriage where her husband would beat her when drinking a lot. She had another son, and while trying to raise the boys, after a divorce, her mother and sisters moved in and out several times as her father never supported them.

Sara Lin had been studying Science of Mind for several years, learning to pray and meditate. She had been trying to contact her spiritual guides, when one night in 1966, "The door opened and instead of dear ones, there were these hideous voices trying to control. At first I was so frightened that at times I would black out. I finally took a stand and when I did, the fear disappeared but they did not. Many tried to help and I tried everything I knew but to no avail."

During Sara Lin's stay, we and our group worked in depth with her and Sara Lin worked diligently herself, forgiving these forces and forgiving herself for having worked with them. She felt great relief while she was here, but had barely been home for a month when she contacted me again.

She wrote, "What does confuse me is that frequently a male voice speaks to me and tells me in no uncertain terms that he is Lucifer. He says he has frequently been put out but always manages to break back in. He also says it is his job to make me fall and he will continue to contest me. He also says I have fought him for many years. His voice, which is quite clear, is always preceded by a flash of light at my right. He also says he is not human and cannot be hurt. Is this just another thoughtform?"

It was then that we began to understand what was really going on — what was the root cause of these attacks. Although the other names she had received including the "Daddy" group had been very actively attacking her, they were all under the Luciferian headquarters. We did not feel this was actually the fallen God, "Lucifer", but was a Luciferian who took that name for identity.

Sara Lin continued to have attacks from time to time and each time we worked to clear any invading D.E.s that often slipped in and also to help to free her from the Luciferian power. Several years before we had suggested that she contact a "Bach Flower" practitioner we knew, but she phoned she had not done so, and that using love and forgiveness seemed to open her up more. We

91

also discovered another of her attackers had been a black magician in the cult of Diana in early Greece where Sara Lin had been a priestess. There were many, many dark ties to be severed and dissolved.

In June of 1982, another cry for help came because of a deep attack.

"Through desperate confrontation", she wrote, "he has let his name out as 'Rasputin'. My friend says Rasputin was a black priest who tried to control Catherine the Great of Russia" (Actually it was the Tsarina Alexandra, not Catherine) "and was finally assassinated, but not before he caused great misery. My friend thinks I knew him in another life or that one. This entity says he hates women and that he cursed me on his death bed. That he is well versed in black magic is all too true. They constantly put out black threads for control."

Since Rasputin was an actual discarnate entity, we did a release and called on the In-God-We-Trust angels to put him in their net of golden light and take him to the "Fifth Sun" where he would have to stay until he learned God's law. We also asked that the curse be dissolved and consumed.

In the fall of 1982 we received another desperate request for help and kept another three-day vigil, from 10/29 to 11/1, in which we called to Jesus Christ, Archangel Michael, the Master "R" and the Golden Legions of Light to seize and bind "A" known to Sara Lin as "Daddy" and his cohorts and take them out of the galaxy. We also placed Sara Lin's picture under a violet lamp day and night for four days in this protective, transmuting light.

Sara Lin replied to thank us for our "wonderful letter" and said she had had a few good days, but was still feeling her life energy being drained from her back, back of head, neck and ear. She added that beside the Luciferians and the black magicians, there were the "Pan" or "Satyr" forces. She had not mentioned the latter before.

She added, "When the Satyr or Pan-like creatures leave, taking with them their elementals, the others have a much harder time getting to me. My hearing (inner) is growing and it annoys them that I hear them plot and conspire. It is all for control to make me fall and to provide an energy source for them."

We had given Sara Lin many powerful mantras to use, among

them the most powerful original Hebrew, "Kadoish, Kadoish, Kadoish, Adonai Sabbaoth" meaning Holy, Holy, Holy is the Lord God of Hosts.4 This is very sacred and can be used for protection of one's self and family and to deter the dark brotherhood.

Sara Lin, who was trying very hard to help herself, then wrote" "I have such a heartfelt shame for causing you so much trouble and accomplishing so little for myself. I care naught anymore but I grieve for teachers and dear ones who have worked so hard to free me who have been unable to free myself. May God bless all of you eternally for all of your heartfelt love and devotion. I no longer kid myself. I can count on both my hands the days I have truly been totally free from some form of attachment in the past five or six years. Don't worry about it – I'll keep on as long as I can... I guess it isn't whether you win or lose, but how long you play the game, and I'll fight them until I die."

But Sara Lin did not give up and we continued to pray for her and check her for D.E.s from time to time, and had given her some banishing rituals to use. Then a phone call came from a friend in another state who had had a similar problem and told us how she overcame it. So we wrote Sara Lin:

"We understand there are other portions of ourselves living in different frequencies. Since time is only relevant on this planet, there is no time in other dimensions so all the selves we have ever been are still functioning and are continuing to do what they did in what we call a 'past life'. Our friend, Joan, says these selves or portions of us are called 'zans', singular, zan. She has a zan who was working with the evil forces and had been attacking her in many ways. Joan began to talk to her and try to rehabilitate her, telling her she wanted to help her evolve and make progress. At first, Z wouldn't listen and was worse than ever, so Joan locked her up in a cage (psychic) with the help of the angels, until she finally agreed to listen. It took five years, but she has been completely changed and is helping Joan now in the light.

"Sara Lin, we know you have worked with the Luciferian group in the past and that 'self' is still functioning. We had not been aware of this before and we are so grateful for this new light. You gave me the name of a female in the group one time... this could be the one and is what you must find out. It could be male although I have the feeling it's female. Give this zan a name and start working with it, with the help of the Christ and your Guides. No one can do this for you. And when the others attack you, above all, do not get angry or resentful. They can use that energy. Joan said she started loving them and told them so. (This made Sara Lin's attackers furious!)

"When they attack, immediately throw up a flaming blue cross *on that spot or spots.* Joan said to call to Archangel Raphael because He is in charge of air and Lucifer is an air spirit... The color to use is *blue* and burn a blue candle, if you wish. Call also to Christ and the other archangels, but chiefly to Raphael."

Working on her zan seemed to do a lot for Sara Lin and she wrote some time later, "Well bless you dear one for all your work. I feel if I could just get this neck and back of head sealed up, it would do the trick." In checking recently we found that these were the *terminal* points of an "implant" at the base of the spine. This was dissolved and consumed and the spot drained and filled with light. In a powerful class session we asked that the whole group be taken out of our solar system and that the spot they had occupied in the astral realm be cleansed and filled with light.

The reader may question why such a long period of time was involved with so many, many sessions of work. "Isn't God all-powerful? Couldn't it all have been done instantaneously"? Of course, the answer is yes. But the human aspect was involved. Sara Lin had been told at the outset to use "love" but felt she could not, that they were beyond the reach of love.

It is important to remember that love, *divine love* is the most powerful force in the universe! It is the cohesive power of love that holds the stars and planets in their orbits. But it must be used and sent *impersonally* without feeling, as it is God's love and not our personal love. When it reaches its destination and is accepted, its power works to change and uplift. But when the love is sent to an evil source and is not accepted, it goes back to the sender, fortified and expanded, creating a forcefield of protection which the evil ones cannot penetrate.

Sara Lin had willingly worked with these satanic groups for several lifetimes and they considered her one of them. Strong aka cords had been built between them that only she could break. These were reinforced by their continuous draining of her energy, especially from the Kundalini area, which they used. Also, since she was able to see and hear on the astral level to an increasing degree, this awareness of them kept drawing her back into their whirlpool of influence.

The power of thought is so strong and we feel that she often drew them to her just by thinking of them. Every time they were removed, it would be only a matter of days before they were back. So we began to realize that this was a do-it-yourself job that only she could accomplish, but she had to build up her spiritual strength to do it. Although we became aware of this early in the work, we could keep her clear of the D.E.s and demons that managed to attach to her aura from time to time. We also made powerful calls for angelic forces to keep these evil powers away from her. This they were able to do for short periods to give her respite.

Sara Lin was involved with a gigantic struggle between the forces of evil and the powers of Light and was well aware of it. Her steadfast determination to overcome and her strong faith in God through it all will be inscribed in her Book of Life in flaming letters of gold!

CHAPTER 9

Poltergeists, Demons, and Elementals

Poltergeists are unruly, mischievous entities who delight in playing pranks. These are the ones that knock on the walls or furniture, hide things only to have them suddenly reappear, and cause many other unaccountable, exasperating problems.

However, sometimes after the death of a dear one in the home, he or she will knock or throw some personal item on the floor or some other activity to get one's attention. He wants the grieving ones to know he is all right and is there with them. Or he may try to show where a lost will was kept or other personal papers. This would not be classed as poltergeist activity.

A most unusual case was the experience of Eleanore T., where over a period of years, her possessions, usually jewelry, would disappear and often reappear. She wrote to ask for help and described some of the activity as follows:

"It started many years ago when a box of turquoise (in a shoe box) disappeared. Later it was replaced... A very large gold bracelet disappeared for many months. One day I opened my jewel box and it materialized while I was looking at it. I have a gold 'Cross' pen which dropped in the commissary. It disappeared on the way down, however, I heard it drop. The cashier also heard it, but we could not find it."

She said several dresses had disappeared but one was later found hanging in the closet. Her wedding band of twisted pink and green gold and her special gold earrings were taken and later returned. She also mentioned many other pieces of jewelry as well as many pairs of prescription glasses. "One time", she added, "when my last pair was taken, I was mad. I was riding a stationary bike and they suddenly fell in front of the bike!"

We found eighteen D.E.s in Eleanore's home, four of whom were poltergeists. When these forces were all removed, along with some D.E.s from her aura, this very disturbing activity stopped.

Georgia wrote, "This week I've lost two sets of keys in the house. The first set I haven't found yet. The second set, I found exactly where I dropped them on the bed, but where they seemed to disappear. They were not there – then they were! Later I was measuring packages for the U.P.S. and the tape measure disappeared. When I didn't get upset, there it was."

Before we had time to do an analysis for her, she wrote again: "In filling a sugar bowl, I spilled (without knowing how) sugar all over the floor. I cleaned that up. A neighbor dropped in for tea (I used some English tea I had been hoarding) and opened the taped box upside down, pouring the loose tea all over the floor. I cleaned that up.

"When I went to dinner at a cafeteria, I bought a serving of chicken and dumplings to take out. When I came into the house, I didn't turn the light on – it's a small house and I know it well. But I had just returned from a short trip and left my suitcases in the hall. I fell and the chicken and dumplings were spewed all over the carpet."

Georgia felt one accident might have happened normally but three in one day was pretty weird. We checked and found that there were seventeen D.E.s in the house and three of them were poltergeists. We felt that these spirits were behaving like pet animals often do when left alone a long time. They were either unhappy that she had gone away or angry because she came back! Anyway, the home was cleared and there were no more problems.

❖ ❖ ❖

Louise had lost her whole set of keys including those for the house, car, and post office box. Friends had been visiting for several days and had left that morning for their home in the east. After searching everywhere, she concluded the woman might have picked them up by mistake and put them in her purse. She contacted them as soon as they reached their destination but they had no knowledge of them. Duplicate keys had to be made, and then sometime later she realized that the keys to the storage room and a workshop had disappeared. These keys were on a different ring and fortunately both doors were unlocked. Although the first set of keys was never found, one morning two years later, Louise was casually walking around the outside of the carport and before she stepped on the cement floor, something caught her eye in the dust. There were the two keys that had been missing! She had walked there many times and no keys; also, if they had been there through all the rain and snow, they would have been dirty and dull. But these keys were shiny and clean, and even the string they were attached to was not soiled.

When Louise told us of this experience, we found that there were indeed poltergeists on the grounds, but not in the home – it was clear. Somehow they decided it would be a clever trick to return the keys! Our Indian runners took them away to another plane of consciousness.

✧   ✧   ✧

Although the translators of the King James version of the Bible used the term "demons" for all negative invisible creatures, we use the term for a specific kind of manifestation. Demons are evil thoughtforms created by masters of black magic to do their bidding. Most of them were created ages ago by the black adepts and evil priesthood as servants or slaves, sent out to work various types of malicious deeds. Most of the creators are long gone but the demons are still existing, feeding on the energy they can obtain from human beings.

Since demons are creations of human thought, they have no soul or eternal spark as with a discarnate entity. Consequently, it is possible to have them dissolved and consumed and their energy transmuted. We call to the angels of the Violet Flame to do this and to release the transmuted energy for good.

We could not find in our files any specific cases where only demons were present, but there are hundreds of instances where both D.E.s and demons were found, some of which are mentioned in this book.

Elementals are the nature spirits of earth (elves, fairies, gnomes), air (sylphs), fire (salamanders), and water (undines). Somehow one of these little invisible beings of the second density can become attached to one of the inner bodies of a human, usually the emotional. They can be very mischievous and make a child difficult to handle. Almost always they attach to children, possibly because children are so much closer to nature than are adults. These little elementals can also attach to or enter animals, making them act strange and abnormal.

When little Linda P. was only three years old, we were visiting in the home. She was always into mischief, her mother said, and they had to watch her every moment. While we were there, she managed to get into the bathroom (door was kept shut), pull a stool up to the washbowl and turn on the water. No one knew she was in there until the water started to run into the hallway and living room! Another time she climbed up to get the can of talcum powder and spilled it all over.

One might say that most small children are into everything, but Linda was more so! She paid no attention to what she was told and all "No-No's" were especially enchanting. She really had a wicked gleam in her eye.

We did an analysis for Linda and found there was indeed an elemental on her emotional body. When this was removed and sent back to the elemental kingdom for training and discipline, Linda became a changed child – almost overnight! The next time we saw her, she was happily playing with her toys or with neighbor children, did what she was asked to do, and her mother said she was no trouble at all.

When Barbara sent her picture for us to do an analysis, she was holding her tabby cat. In doing the work for Barbara, we felt impressed to check the cat – we just had a funny feeling about that cat! So we checked the cat and there was an elemental attachment which was released. When we mentioned this to Barbara, she wrote back later: "Ever since you checked my kitty, he has been so changed – truly a love!"

Under the heading of elementals, we wish to add that most of them do their work faithfully and well. It is only a very few that fall down on the job or somehow become attached to humans or animals. One must remember that life is intelligent regardless of the density, although the degree of intelligence is less in denser materials such as rocks and coal. Crystals contain a high degree of elemental intelligence; in fact, these little beings are found in gases,

99

air, flames, chemicals as well as solids – they are the servants that perform the various functions of their makeup. They work under the direction of great elemental over-lords called "Devas". One should also be aware of the fact that the elementals get their energy from the emotions and feelings of human beings. They cannot think or discriminate but take what is given them to use; be it anger, hatred, or fear. So it behooves us to send love and joy to them and to keep our own emotions under control!

A very unusual case we had recently was that of an elemental attachment on a basic self, which is also an elemental! Abby is a spiritually-trained worker and counselor who was practicing to become proficient with the pendulum. But it simply wouldn't work right, giving far-fetched and very unreasonable answers. In desperation, she asked us to check and we found an elemental attachment on her basic self. After this was removed, her pendulum began to work satisfactorily.

When an elemental is released for whatever reason, it is sent back to the elemental kingdom to which it belongs for rehabilitation and training.

CHAPTER 10

Supra-physical Shells

We first became aware of what we call "supraphysical shells" after reading the book, *Many Lifetimes* by Denys Kelsey and Joan Grant. They called it a supra-physical "body" and maintained that:
"The body of every individual has a physical and a supra-physical component; and when the energy-exchange between these two components ceases to exist, the physical body dies. But the supra-physical body does not die. It cannot die; for the simple reason that it consists of an order of matter which is not subject to the process which we call 'death', a process during which the physical particles integrated by an energy-field have become inactive."

They add that, "Many apparently irrational fears have their origin in some painful episode experienced by an earlier supra-physical which the current body is determined not to repeat."

And they go on to say that these supra-physical components can maintain an independent identity as long as the personality gives them sufficient energy.

"But if any of them contains an undue amount of energy, which it cannot or will not release, this energy can cause trouble to the current personality; or to a later one in the same series."

It seems now that many unusual habits or fears for which there is no logical explanation, can be traced to traumatic experiences in early childhood or a still earlier personality in a former life. What Kelsey and Grant call the "supra-physical body" is generally known in metaphysical parlance as the "etheric body", the exact duplicate of the physical body in a higher frequency. It surrounds the physical body and extends several inches out from it. We find that a habit, fear, or emotional behavior pattern that has been deeply imprinted in the etheric body forms a type of calcified matter or a shell attached to that body. We call this a "supraphysical shell". Usually, these shells disintegrate between lives, but if there has been an excessive amount of emotion in a given situation, the shell does not disintegrate but remains energized and is magnetically drawn to the body at birth. We find these shells can be dissolved and transmuted by the angels of the Violet Flame.

Joan Grant relates her own experience of not being able to sit up in bed and drink or take nourishment when ill. She had to lie flat with her head on the side and drink through a straw or be fed by spoon. She insisted she couldn't swallow any other way, much to her husband's annoyance. He persuaded her to go back to her childhood and try to find the cause of this strange habit.

Instead, she suddenly found herself in a former life where she had been thrown from a horse and was paralyzed from the neck down. The only way she could be fed was in the above fashion, and this had impressed itself in her present etheric body. As soon as she became aware of the cause, she was able to dissolve the old energy and was never bothered again.

It is our belief that many cases of alcoholism are caused by supra-physical shells from a former life where the subjects were being operated on without anesthetic, in the Crimean War, the Civil War, and others where they ran out of anesthetic. The wounded soldier would be given large quantities of alcohol before an amputation or other surgery. In many cases, they were in short supply and there was not enough whiskey to put the patient to sleep, and he would die screaming and crying for more whiskey. Needless to say, he would bring back into the next life this intense desire for alcohol.

We have had several cases of this nature and after the patient understood why he had such a craving, and the shell was dissolved, the desire for drinking alcohol left him.

Joan L. was suffering from an emotional problem known as "Agoraphobia", which is a term used to denote fear of open or public places. She was afraid to go anywhere in public, even the grocery store, and was terrified of being anywhere outside her home.

We found that she had some D.E.s inside and outside the aura that were giving her some emotional and physical problems, but she also had a supra-physical shell from her last lifetime in which these old fears were so deeply ingrained in that previous life, they had formed a shell which had attached to her present body causing many difficulties that neither she nor her doctors could understand.

A release was done for the D.E.s, but in the case of the supra-physical shell, we called to the angels of the Violet flame to dissolve and consume every vestige of it, transmuting the energy into light.

After Joan received our letter, she wrote that on the evening of the release (about an hour after the completion),"My husband and I both knew there were spirits or Spirit in our living room. The next morning just before awakening I felt a whitish, yellowish glow around me. Two days later a few friends came over and both noticed a difference in my looks. They described it as my face 'being opened'.

"I have also noticed when I went into the bank (which is always accompanied by anxiety), I felt rather relaxed. I haven't gone anywhere alone as yet. I also went for a long walk with my husband (also difficult for me), and it was generally comfortable. I sat on a bench and read my prayer and it was consoling. (I realize) it will take time to reprogram."

When Herman N.'s friend sent us a request for help for him, she told us that he had been an intelligent, competent, and self-sufficient individual but, "The last two years I have watched this man lose his sense of logic, his competence is on the decline, his self-confidence and his job. The deterioration started with a physical which diagnosed Hodgkin's disease and he was given two years to live... A year later, it was determined to be an erroneous diagnosis and that he had Bright's disease instead.

"I have seen this man's body shake so badly he couldn't hold a cup of coffee or sign his name. He goes for days without eating, and the medication ruins his ability to think clearly, which is his livelihood. His drinking has increased tremendously. His equilibrium is so poor he rarely leaves the apartment except for necessities."

We were also told that Herman had returned to the area to care for his mother about five years previously. She had a severe heart condition, arthritis, and was developing cataracts.

Our analysis showed fourteen D.E.s, one inside the physical and the rest inside and outside the aura. They were affecting him, emotionally and physically, but most important, there were three supra-physical shells from previous lives, as well as a mind control from his mother, who was afraid he might leave her. There were also seventeen D.E.s in their home.

At the time of release, the mind control was broken and one supra-physical shell was dissolved. The remaining two were dissolved at the end of four months, which was the restoration period.

His friend wrote about a month after the release:

"On the day you were working with him, we were at a cabin in the mountains for the weekend. About 10:30 pm. he experienced severe pain in the kidney area and he used what appeared to be sheer willpower to force it to subside. There was a great deal of rest and relaxation while we were there, however, he did complain of a headache on Sunday — something he very rarely has.

"Since that time and up until last week, there has been an attitude of enthusiasm for improved eating habits, his work, and life in general. He was discussing things to be done next year... and he is talking of spending more time in the mountains and not pushing himself so hard. Needless to say, this pleases me tremendously for I believe he has forgotten how to play and/or relax. I am trying very hard to keep only positive thoughts for his welfare... Again, thank you for your time and consideration. I know your prayers and thoughts have proved to be beneficial for us both."

Since we heard no more about Herman, we assume he continued to improve.

❖   ❖   ❖

Theo was a student on the spiritual path with a very deep commitment to God and God's will in his life. Yet there were many stumbling blocks in his way, such as hearing "astral conversations",

104

being aware of D.E.s at times, as well as being unsure of the source of his guidance. He suffered daily from headaches as well as an extreme cold spot at the base of his skull, and was very susceptible to drafts.

We found eight D.E.s of a very negative nature inside and outside the aura as well as a supra-physical shell on the emotional body. It was noted that the psychic door at the base of the skull was open and that was causing the "cold spot". After this door was closed and healed, the cold spot disappeared.

The supra-physical shell related to extreme input of emotional energy in a former life but we were unable to determine just how it was affecting him. However, after the release, all the above symptoms disappeared.

Theo wrote also that he had a new job and it was the biggest challenge he had faced, and "Your work on me has helped this effort exceedingly".

❖ ❖ ❖

Mrs. P. asked us to do some work for her daughter. Mary, age twenty, had extreme personality problems and had become unkempt and careless about her person. We found a deep infiltration of eleven D.E.s, some inside the body and the rest inside the aura. Her High Self was blocked and there were no spiritual guides. Inner stress was extremely high and self-evaluation, willpower, and determination were all below average.

After the release, inner stress went down to normal, self-evaluation was still somewhat below average, but willpower and determination had returned to average. Her High Self was in contact and she had been given four spiritual guides.

Mary's mother wrote to say that the evening of the release she began to change: "Mary volunteered to do one or two things for me, and she began to smile. She had been sullen and full of complaints, but tonight she has even begun to laugh a little. She has never learned to help people; it has never come spontaneously to offer assistance in even the simplest situation. She has had to be told to help. Yet, when it came time to think of work, she has had one compelling intention – to take care of a family, cook, clean, wash, and take care of the children. It is as if something is impelling her irresistibly into positions where she must serve.

"Mary refuses any effort to help her with physical treatment and she has never admitted to me or anyone else that she had any problems of any kind. But yet she seems so unhappy, so bored, yet frustrated to the point of explosion at times. She cannot like herself for she has permitted herself to get overweight and unkempt."

After we received the above letter a month later, we did another analysis for Mary, as we had just learned about the existence of supra-physical shells and had the feeling this might be part of her problem. Indeed, we found there were two of them influencing her, but were only given permission to release one, as the other was too deeply ingrained in her emotional body and would have to be gradually prepared for removal. There were also seven new D.E.s on the outside of the aura. Interestingly, we found she had an emotional age of ten, which went up to seventeen after the release.

Two months later we received another report, so wonderfully encouraging. Mary had begun a live-in job taking care of two little girls, two horses, two dogs, chickens, and a house while the mother worked. Her mother commented, "I have only seen her briefly twice since she started and she seems very happy and is enjoying it. This weekend she went on a little vacation with a friend and brought back a gift for me, one for her employer and a shirt for each little girl.

"Recently her employer (stopped by) spoke in such glowing terms of Mary – her efficiency, her reliability, her prompt response to every direction – it was hard to believe she was talking about Mary! Yes, I know she is changing and this job away from home is very good. I do thank you for your great contribution in making all this possible. God does bring the right people together in the right way, in the right time."

Four months after the first release, we were given permission (by our High Self) to remove the second supra-physical shell. Her mother had written: "Mary is now showing the true nature of this remaining shell and it is not an agreeable personality. I'm glad we had plastic plates on Tuesday evening or they would have been in pieces!"

After this work was done, as well as the removal of four new D.E.s that had attached outside the aura, which had been seriously weakened, we worked again on healing and sealing the aura in light. After this second shell was removed, we received glowing reports from time to time of Mary's very positive personality changes and plans for her life. As far as we know, Mary continued to improve until her former fears were completely dissipated.

It would appear that this concept of emotional shells being dissolved could be quite a breakthrough in the field of Psychiatry if accepted. Not only are these shells usually created in previous lifetimes, but they can also be formed from traumatic experiences in early childhood.

However, the effect or manifestation of a shell does not always occur early in life. Often, it is triggered later by an illness or intense emotional experience which re-activates it.

It is our understanding that the etheric body contains the blueprint or pattern for the entire physical body so that everything that takes place in the physical, occurs first in the etheric, and then gradually develops in the physical. This means that diseases as well as healings begin in the etheric or supra-physical body. Therefore, by removing the emotional energy that was originally put into the shell and disintegrating it, the restored pattern would then filter down into the physical body where the intelligence in the appropriate cells and nerve impulses should begin to change accordingly.

CHAPTER 11

Rock And Roll Music

Adherents of contemporary popular music may not wish to consider any adverse comments about its effects, but we feel the following information must be given and the reader is free to make his own decisions. We do not wish to castigate all rock music – there are a few compositions that do not conform to the trend, some of the "soft rock" – but the majority of it can be very destructive to the cell structure of the brain and body as well as dulling one's sensitivity to a higher type of music. Of more importance is the fact that the constant bombardment tends to weaken the auric field and allow the attachment of D.E.s and demonic forces which are drawn by the beat and sound of rock music.

Most contemporary writers seem to be composing rhythmic noise which we feel should never be construed as "music"; monstrous crescendos of discordant confusion jangle the nerves and stupefy the senses, in the classical field as well as the popular.

In the entertainment world, we have enthroned the mediocre or worse than mediocre – dazed with drugs, untrained and untalented for the most part, but setting the pace for our contemporary culture or lack of it!

The beat of rock music and the inane repetition of a few bars over and over are based on some of the most primitive emotion-inciting concepts. Much of the singing, which often builds up to screaming, shrieking, and yelling is very primitive also. Then the volume is turned so high that it blasts the eardrums of the listeners, causing extensive hearing damage. The musicians themselves, as well as the stage crew, wear earplugs!

On stage, the flashing colored lights with their constant on-off syndrome play on the brain, through the eyes, and have a hypnotic effect on the thinking process thereby putting the emotions under complete control of the music. These lights are computer-programmed to a certain sequence.

Most parents and older adults have paid little or no attention to the lyrics of rock music. There are insidious references to drugs and sex, sometimes in code words that only teenagers would understand, and even injunctions like "Kill your mother" which are repeated so fast as to be not understandable, but the meaning is hammered subtly into the subconscious mind in constant repetition. *Think about this!*

We understand that the lower astral realms are very closely interpenetrating earth more than ever before, with the evil entities of those realms trying to influence and attach themselves to human beings. The young people are especially vulnerable because they open themselves up through drugs, alcohol, sex (one way to take on the partner's D.E.s), pornography in any media, and especially listening to the beat of rock music. Hard rock and punk rock are the most destructive of all, having a greater deteriorating effect on the brain cells as well as the emotional body.

Soft rock or disco music, usually played for dancing, are not as detrimental as hard rock, but there is a certain hypnotic, primitive effect in moving to the beat as shown on the faces of those who are participating. Look at them on television! The dancers never smile or look like they're having fun but nearly always wear dead-pan or even sullen expressions which are also seen on the faces of savages dancing in the African jungle! In fact the whole concept of rock music is right out of the jungle.

In the second volume of her book, *I Will Arise*, Paola Hugh comments: "Certain types of music now prevalent contain a rhythmic measure that is disintegrating to the brain cells, and thence violently disruptive. This also is promulgation of dark forces."[6]

Confirmation of this was given us recently regarding a Christian minister who had followed a well-known rock band all over Europe making recordings, in the early days of rock. This particular group wrote their own music and the leader admitted to the minister that he had been approached and offered large sums of money if he would include a *certain type bar of music in every song he wrote,* which he did. Others followed suit, some probably unaware of what they were doing, but most likely other writers were approached also. We were told that nefarious forces were behind the whole program in order to degrade the minds of our young people.

The minister later had scientific experiments made with mice and it was found that the brain cells did indeed deteriorate when bombarded by his recordings of this music. The mice went completely berserk!

There have been several documented, controlled experiments made which definitely show the detrimental effects of rock and roll music on plants.[7] The plants exposed to classical music grew and thrived; those exposed to rock music drooped and died.

We have no documentation on how many of the children and young people for whom we have worked, listened regularly to rock and roll music, but most have been warned. We do know that it tends to lower the vibrations of the auric protective sheath and open it so that evil discarnate entities and demons, drawn by the sound, can enter.

Although country music cannot be classed as spiritually or culturally uplifting, it does not have the destructive beat and chord progression. Although some consider it to be deleterious, we cannot concur in this conclusion.

The following information was taken from a taped lecture by John Todd, and we leave it up to the reader to draw his own conclusions and read it with an open mind, considering the possibilities. Some younger people feel that he comes across much too strong and that his claims are not entirely true. However, even if they are extreme, his life has been threatened and several attempts made on it, so his expose may be valid.

John Todd (his pseudonym) is a former male witch and member of the High Council of Thirteen, who became converted to Christianity. He said in his lecture that Zodiac Productions owns about ninety-five percent of the contracts for rock and country musicians in the United States. Todd worked for them before becoming a Christian.

He claims that all major record companies have a "Coven Room" set up – a temple room with a pentagram on the floor, an alter with candles and incense. After a recording session, a coven of witches comes in and lays hands on the master tape before it is produced and a spell is cast on every record.

"A spell is an order to demons", he explained, "and demons are ordered out with every record that comes off the press... The only reason for rock music is to control people!

"Several years ago, churches began preaching against rock and roll music and really scared the record companies", Todd continued. "The churches saw how it caused rebellion, drug intake, free love, and so on. The record companies spent eight million dollars to build a record company, Maranatha Industries, to create 'Jesus Rock'. This has the same effect as the other rock and country songs – it's in the music."

We have noted the unfortunate trend in Christian music to imitate the contemporary songs as well as their way of singing and playing. This can have nothing but a deteriorating effect on the singers and players, as well as the listeners. We know of a church that has dispensed with its organ and relies entirely on guitars and this questionable type of music for its Sunday morning and other services. One should note that religious music has always been different from street music until the present time.

"Every witch knows", Todd continued, "and I know from working at Zodiac Music Company, that a rock song is a spell."

He said the KISS group, when asked about the strange name, replied, "We were ordered to use that name. We're rock singers second, we're ministers first – ordained in the Satanic Brotherhood of America." They also said they were all homosexuals, and that KISS stands for K-ings I-n S-atanic S-ervice. They all showed their ministerial cards!

Real religious music has great power. Todd said there are about five Christian groups whose music witches are forbidden to listen to, and the "Gaithers'" music is on top of the list.

"Parents", continued Todd, "you are urged not to allow those records in your children's hands. *burn them!* The children would not be rebellious or run away from home if you had not bought them that music. Don't wait a week, don't ask their permission. You are the one who owns it – it's your house. Don't throw it out or give it away — *burn it!* Burning breaks the spell."

However, we have been told that records should not be burned as poisonous gases can result and be dangerous. In that case, it would be advisable to break them in pieces and place in the trash.

Recently we happened to tune in to a talk-show on television on which rock and roll music was being discussed and the guests on the platform were four rock musicians. We were surprised to hear members of the audience bring out nearly everything we have mentioned.

One woman said, "Parents, you're not listening — you don't know what's coming on!" Several young people acknowledged the hidden messages and meanings in the lyrics but felt it wasn't hurting them. Two young girls both said that they were "good girls" and had been brought up right and would never "have a baby" or take drugs, so the music and lyrics were not affecting them.

A young man said that if you tell teenagers what the lyrics are doing to them — urging them to take drugs, have sex, etc., they won't believe you anyway. They think your parents don't know anything and will deliberately do just the opposite.

A mature woman who had been a popular singer said to stop blaming parents, and reminded the rock musicians about their moral responsibility to the audience — the effect their lives and habits have on the kids. The rock stars on stage didn't feel this was their responsibility at all and that some of the entertainers took drugs in about the same proportion as those of the audience. The woman went on to say that she felt soft rock was ok but punk rock and hard rock — "Forget it, it's degenerate"!

Someone brought up the fact that all those involved in this field are out to make money and they don't care how they make it or what the effects are. One of the musicians agreed that of course they wanted to make money. Doesn't everyone?

In closing, someone asked, "Whatever happened to *beautiful* music?" We wonder, too.

CHAPTER 12

Psychic Tools — Channeling, Ouija Board, Hypnosis

The verb "to channel" among most esoteric or metaphysical groups, means to give over one's voice for the use of a discarnate being — all the way from the lower astral realm to the high spiritual realms where the Great White Brotherhood and the Spiritual Hierarchy of our planet reside, and even beings from other solar systems at times.

There are several ways to channel of which one is to go into a trance state in which the being takes over the body completely, using a different voice, different mannerisms and gestures, and even on occasion, changing the facial features of the channel to a degree. The real personality is unaware of what is being said and is in a deep, unconscious sleep state as in a dream. A being of good moral caliber will protect the channel and see that the aura is closed after he leaves. And the channel, as well, should do everything in his power to protect himself. It is very simple for a discarnate entity to slip in if a trance channel is not fully protected or has not lifted his consciousness high enough.

We have been advised that as a rule the highest spiritual teachers do not come through a trance channel because it could be dangerous to his lower bodies, as their vibration is too high to come down through a physical medium. However, in some cases, the teacher bringing through the message is an advanced soul giving much needed information so comes through a higher astral go-between or if the person in trance has been carefully trained on the inner planes to go out of the body and allow the incoming teacher to alter the frequencies, he may speak directly through him. Some channels have even been trained in previous lifetimes. The late Edgar Cayce, called "The Sleeping Prophet", apparently channeled a higher part of himself (High Self) and was very spiritually oriented. The method most preferred is what some call "telepathic" channeling and this is where the channel goes into a type of deep meditation, blocking out his own thoughts and raising his consciousness to the higher mental or Christ plane, and by-passing the astral plane. Thus he makes a higher connection, allowing an entity of a high spiritual level to impress his higher mind. This is also called "overshadowing". The channel is awake and aware of what is being said, although in a very detached manner. Often when a high spiritual being is speaking, those in the audience can see a glow of light around the channel and feel the greatly enhanced vibrations of love and blessing.

Another type of channeling is through writing by hand or on the typewriter. Many wonderful books have been written in this manner as well as lessons and messages for personal guidance. When this takes place, the receiver sits with notebook in hand or at the typewriter and goes into the above mentioned deep meditation and *protection*, waiting for the dictation to begin.

Automatic writing is something to be avoided like the plague! This is when another force takes over the hand of the writer, guiding each letter forcibly so the writer has no control of his hand and in time may be completely at the mercy of lower discarnates.

An acquaintance was showing several of us how she did automatic writing one time. First she made wide scrawls and circles which finally condensed to a legible handwriting of strange, meaningless phrases which she proceeded to interpret. Suddenly, her eyes became very bulgy-looking and her throat was seized by a kind of paralysis, and then a low, sepulchral voice began to speak through her. It said, "I have been moldering in the grave for many, many years." We were all too young and inexperienced to know what was going on, so we giggled and exclaimed, "Margie, what's the matter with you? Why are you talking so funny?"

Finally we began to realize it was a demonic force and we told it in the Name of Jesus Christ to get out of there and leave Margie alone. It apparently left, but we had learned our lesson — *not* to try automatic writing!

The lower astral realm is filled with D.E.s who desire to come through with their own brand of ego-oriented information, often parading under the names of well-known people of the past or even Ascended Masters, including Jesus. We have proved beyond doubt that there is a group or groups of impostors on the lower astral levels who have assumed the names of higher masters and obligingly give spurious messages to the gullible channel who has neither protected himself or raised his consciousness.

Following is an excerpt from a letter written by a dear friend and teacher to a mutual acquaintance who felt she had become a channel:

"The *path* is a razor's edge – it is sometimes hard to remember this if we are anxious for growth and we want to move on quickly. Perhaps if you will try to remember just where you were this time last year you might see why I feel I should definitely caution you at this time. You are quite new at the integration process of your physical, emotional and mental bodies and I have found from my own personal experience that this job is never finished – as soon as you think you have it all together, another challenge hits you and you integrate on yet another level.

"Early in my esoteric training and studies we were cautioned over and over about channeling of mediums and most psychics. We were given meditation work and exercises to help us contact our own Higher Consciousness to build the bridge from the personality to the soul. As you know, this is called the Antahkarana, and I'm sure we have been working on it for many lives. The personality has a tendency to be a runaway horse and must be brought into control so that the messages from the soul – and eventually from pure Spirit – are not garbled or distorted. You have had much emotion to contend with... and with all of us, that emotional body has to be as still as a windless pond for us to get clear messages... We have been helped greatly by the Flower Remedies and I salute Dr. Bach very often", she continued.

"By this time you must realize that I am reluctant to accept some of the messages your group have received. I don't believe you can be initiated into the Great White Brotherhood on the physical plane. This kind of thing can be dangerous, and we are told to *test each spirit*. Human beings in their eagerness are often duped.

One of the main problems with the probationer on the path is glamour. If you will read again the names you were given, it might make you wonder that such an advanced spiritual group would be coming through such faulty human personalities. This is a way to get into trouble as there are many clever impersonators on the astral level.

"Remember, there is only the *eternal now* and we must live in it. We are the sum total of *all* of our lives and experiences and we grow second by second and minute by minute."

Another way to receive messages is through the use of a Ouija Board. In the past we tried to use it to tune into a higher frequency but it didn't work — we received only strange and incorrect answers. We also watched a friend who was convinced her master teacher was coming through. Although many promises were made and future conditions given, nothing came true — even partially!

Working with a Ouija board, especially for amusement, can be very dangerous as it attracts the lower entities and one can soon find himself completely under the control of the force coming in, or even possessed, as the writer observed in one case. These matters should never be considered in the light of entertainment or to try to tune into a higher frequency.

✧ ✧ ✧

Ruth's sister wrote to us for help, saying that Ruth had been hearing voices after having used the Ouija board for several weeks, with her sister and alone. As they were using it, an entity who gave his name as P.G. began to come through, appearing to be one of high intellect and spirituality. As Ruth began to use the board alone, P.G. kept coming in and friends urged her to sever the contact, which she did. But then he took over her hand in automatic writing when she tried to write letters.

Then P.G. confessed that he was not her guide, as he had once informed her. When she stopped writing, he began to speak inside her head — day and night. By now his words were almost always cruel, ugly, hideous and threatening because she was resisting. This continued to the point where she was afraid to sleep in her bedroom and used a small bed near the phone, with the lights on.

Then her sister heard about our work and wrote to us. It is very interesting to note that on the date her sister wrote until the release was completed, Ruth heard no voices — a period of ten days. P.G. seemed aware that she was seeking help.!

When the analysis was done for Ruth, it was found that there were other D.E.s besides P.G., inside and outside the aura, and also quite a few in her home. A release was done, but the next day during the recheck we found that P.G. was still active, although the home was clear and the other D.E.s were gone. The following day another release ritual was performed and we explained to P.G. why he had to go on with our helpers and that he was causing great harm to Ruth as well as to himself. He was finally persuaded to leave, and later she checked out clear.

After they received our letter, the sister wrote that the voices had stopped and that Ruth could now write without having her hand taken over. She was working very hard on herself in prayer, going for walks and spending more time out of doors, and resuming her hobbies. However, she was still fearful that P.G. might return! We told her that he could not come back as the Indian guides had taken him off the earth plane, and that she must not be fearful or even think of him. She vowed she would never try automatic writing or use the Ouija board again.

Whenever a psychic or spirit contact of any kind is being made, one must *test the spirits*. With practice, one can usually tell by the quality of what is coming through, or if the material is extremely repetitious. But one must challenge the spirits in the Name of the Christ – always. This applies to all channels as well, whether in trance or not in trance. However, the Masters do not come though a Ouija board or automatic writing unless it is momentarily in order to introduce the practitioner to higher work. Also, as we mentioned, it is said that the Ascended Masters do not come through a trance channel as they prefer to work telepathically, impressing their messages through the channel's High Self.

The writer was in a meeting one time in which the channel was in trance and the speaker claimed to be a certain teacher from the seventh plane. We silently challenged him in the Name of the Christ and he turned and looked at us straight in the eyes and graciously bowed his (the channel's) head! A very pertinent and beautiful message was given.

One way to challenge, either verbally (if possible) or silently, is to firmly question, "I challenge you in the Name of the Christ.

Do you stand in the light of the Christ?"

A true being of light will thank you and acknowledge his stand, but an imposter may stutter foolishly or just remain silent or leave. He would have to leave as an imposter could not take the light of Christ.

It is so important that the channel has been spiritually trained and prepared for this work, having learned to keep the personality under control, and that he is living up to his highest light. If he is not doing so, but is ego-oriented or money-oriented, he is apt to tune into the spurious beings on the lower planes who are generally highly complimentary and give little pertinent information.

✧ ✧ ✧

Bette asked if we could do an analysis for her but not release her D.E.s because she wanted to keep them! She said one she called Miranda was not good but helped her in "giving readings". We did not do this, but wrote that Miranda was probably doing more harm than good. It is possible for some D.E.s to try to help but since they are generally of a low order or they wouldn't be attached, their information would not be dependable. They like fun and tricks! The term "psychic realm", as it is generally used, is in the astral realm and those dwellers are all of low to medium evolvement. Psychic gifts should not be pursued because they go no higher than the astral, which is the realm of glamour. It is intuition that is of the higher spiritual realm.

Webster's New World Dictionary defines hypnosis as follows:

"A sleeplike condition, psychically induced, usually by another person, in which the subject loses consciousness but responds, with certain limitations, to the suggestions of the hypnotist."

We have heard it said that to allow one's self to be hypnotized by someone else can cause a break between the etheric web and the mental body. This could be extremely dangerous to anyone pursuing higher spiritual disciplines. However, this does not apply to self-hypnosis in which one puts himself into a state of deep meditation and is perfectly cognizant of all that is happening.

Medical and dental hypnosis is not in our field and will not be considered here. However, we should like to mention the fact that we have found several writers who have used the term "hypnosis" and then went on to describe what is usually known as a "guided meditation" or "deep meditation". Both are preceded by putting one's self in the protection of the White Light, then relaxation and a countdown or "going down in an elevator", and in the former procedure the subject is questioned by a trained counselor and the subconscious mind is programmed positively or one is guided into former lives. In the latter deep meditation, one can be alone or in a group, but places himself in a state of awareness where he is open to instruction from his own Higher Self or an Inner-plane Teacher. This can include glimpses of past lives, swirling colors, an inner voice, or nothing at all – just a deep sense of joy and oneness.

In both cases however, the subject is awake and conscious of sounds around him (as though from a distance) like a clock ticking or a telephone ringing – or voices in the room. He is neither asleep nor in a trance, though should he fall asleep, there would be no harm done and he would wake up normally. We feel the term "hypnosis" is a distinct misnomer in both cases and can be misleading.

Deep hypnosis for the purpose of recalling past lives, as in the case of Bridey Murphy[8] could well be damaging, especially when many, many sessions are imposed upon the subject.

A magazine called "Cosmic Awareness Communications"[9] gives another viewpoint in which R.E.E. asks an interesting question:

"A writer purporting afterlife communication says hypnotic subjects must wait on the astral plane after death for the death and arrival of their hypnotist, because a lasting psychic bond fetters them whereby the subject has become a victim and cannot be liberated until the energies are re-balanced on the astral plane. The perils of hypnosis also are recounted by Paramahansa Yogananda who says that it establishes a negative cerebral condition if experienced often."

Cosmic Awareness replies: "This Awareness indicates that this generally is in the affirmative, particularly wherein a subject is continuously put in states of hypnosis under the command of another... An occasional action does not create such bondage and self-hypnosis does not create such bondage. This Awareness indicates also that entities who are linked together by influence on each other, are basically in the same situation. An entity who has strong influence over another, such as a mate, may also expect to find the mate waiting on the other side for that party to pass over. This Awareness indicates that essentially this is the same type of bonding of energies between entities; that the hypnosis action is that wherein one surrenders to the will of another on a temporary or permanent basis."

To quote Yogananda from his book, *Autobiography of a Yogi*, he says: "Hypnotism has been used by physicians in minor operations as a sort of psychical chloroform for persons who might be endangered by an anaesthetic. But a hypnotic state is harmful to those often subjected to it; a negative psychological effect ensues that in time deranges the brain cells. Hypnotism is a trespass into the territory of another's consciousness."[10]

CHAPTER 13

Sex And Homosexuals

Sexual problems seem to be more prevalent than any others. We do not counsel in this field unless it is tied in with the release of discarnate entities; however, we can cite a few cases.

Sharon wrote for releases for herself and live-in partner. They both had a deep infiltration of D.E.s inside and outside the aura that were affecting them emotionally and physically. She asked about having children, and we replied:

"Sharon, I believe you will have children... but especially, don't try until you have the security of marriage. Jesus advocated marriage (Mark 10:6-12). Marriage is much more than a 'piece of paper' and there is something holy and sacred in it that brings peace of mind and security, especially to the woman. She sometimes cannot respond sexually until after the marriage."

Sharon and her man were married shortly after and the next year she sent us a picture of their darling baby boy. The letter was glowing with happiness.

✧ ✧ ✧

Here is a problem that seems to affect some of those who have studied eastern religions and also some Protestant faiths. When two people are happily married, often for years, and one partner suddenly is exposed to a teaching that "sex is wrong" or "should only be used for having children", it becomes a great hardship to the other partner, often leading to divorce.

We wrote to a married man as follows: "Morris, your comment about having 'indulged' in sex recently, leads me to conclude that your attitude toward sex may be slightly warped! I do not know what esoteric school you are with... but after many years of being divorced and learning to re-channel the sex energies, I feel this way about it.

"Everything is spiritual with the right attitude. When God has provided one with a mate, then the sex function should not be considered wrong, bad, or unspiritual. When rightly understood, it can be the most spiritual, beautiful, uplifting relationship – a mortal prelude to the great symphony of soul when man becomes *one* with God. Jesus never condemned sex or marriage.

"He said, 'But from the beginning of the creation God made them male and female. For this cause shall a man leave his father and mother and cleave to his wife. *And they twain shall be one flesh.*' Mark 10:6-8

"There is a beautiful old English marriage ritual in which each party vows, 'and with my body I thee worship!' Do not feel guilty about sex, but dedicate your bodies to God as Living Temples and feel the at-one-ment as truly spiritual. If you are withholding this from Jody, it may be part of her problem and reason for needing psychiatric care. It is very important that you understand her needs as well as your own. We must remember that the sex act is sacred and should not be abused or made a means of just personal satisfaction, however."

✧ ✧ ✧

The following problem is not as unusual as one might think. We have had several.

Vi and Marge were acquaintances who wrote us separately with the same problem – they were both having similar sexual attacks from some unseen force. One of them also heard "voices".

We found D.E.s inside and outside the aura of each and releases were performed. But they continued to have almost constant sexual harassment. In checking Vi in great depth, we found that the entity attacking her was not a discarnate, but was in a physical body – a satanist (or similar). His power was broken many times, but she continued to think about him and listen for him, and was too weak to resist. We asked:

"Have you any idea how these satanists work? They use sexual energy for their nefarious purposes and he, apparently, has learned to project his astral body to you."

We wrote Marge, after receiving another plea for help:

"In rechecking you yesterday, there was no D.E., but there was a hex and mind control, at least an attempted one. Marge, this is something you, yourself, are going to have to overcome. You must learn to be strong and forceful. It is the weak and fearful that they prey upon. You tell me about his attempted sexual contacts, *but what are you doing about it?* Do you order him out in the name of Jesus Christ? Do you call mightily on Jesus Christ for help? We worked in class this morning to break his power, as we have worked many times, and his hold on you is temporarily broken.

"Now, first of all, if you feel the very slightest negative influence or presence, with all the strength of your being, say three times:

'I say to you, in the Name of Jesus Christ, you have no power. Your day is done; your power is now dissolved and consumed from my vibration forever'. Then call to Jesus Christ to clear out that vibration. Repeat the above until it is gone.

"If there is congestion or vibration in the genital area, bring the feeling slowly down to the bottom of your feet, then bring it up slowly to the tail bone, slowly up the backbone to the top of the head; now down again to the feet. (Do not pause in the pelvic area, but keep going.) Do this three times, ending at the top of the head. Then get busy with something else."

Note: It is better to do something active like working in the yard or in the kitchen. If it is at night, get up and watch television or fix a hot drink.

Both of the women were also told how to protect themselves in the tube of white Christ light. It seemed that Marge was doing meditative practices and becoming somewhat clairvoyant. We felt she should be warned of some of the dangers, and wrote:

"Marge, you must learn to challenge the forces, especially those you see when in meditation or otherwise. Because they appear good does not mean they are – usually they are not. Say, 'I challenge you in the name of the Christ! Do you stand in the Christ light?' Be forceful and authoritative. If they are good, they will thank you and stay; if evil, they will melt away.

"I am familiar with (the teaching she mentions) and also various kinds of breathing exercises to raise the kundalini, *but not for you.* Stop all exercises immediately, as well as deep meditation until this thing is cleared up. You are in a very vulnerable state.

The strange feelings you have in the crown chakra, back of the nose, etc. I questioned, but this does not seem to be from malefic forces. The combination of the crown and ajna centers beginning to open plus the satanic force attacking you is too much! The forces of good and evil are tearing you apart. Do nothing of a psychic or occult nature but take the spiritual path of devotion – read devotional books; go deep within yourself, but not into a meditative or subjective state. Anyone going through your experiences could not be mentally or emotionally stable enough for esoteric practices."

We advised Marge to read books like *Letters of the Scattered Brotherhood* by Mary Strong, *The Aquarian Gospel* by Levi, and, of course, the Bible. We heard no more from either of them.

✧ ✧ ✧

This is the only record on file of a woman who admitted to being a homosexual. Marian had been married and had two sons, but her divorced husband had been cruel and vindictive – she was completely through with men. She said that she and another woman were living together in a homosexual relationship and were planning to be legally "married". We had done a release for Don, her son, and replied as follows:

"Marian, you say you are Don's mother and that you plan a 'same sex' marriage to Celia, and that Don does not approve of your actions!

"In love and understanding, I ask you, do you really know what you are doing? And what this is doing to Don and your other son emotionally? Children do not have the mental and emotional maturity to handle or even try to understand this kind of behavior.

"Secondly, I feel your problems are definitely caused by D.E.s which you do have. I checked that much, but was not allowed to check further or do a release unless you ask. You must want it.

"Marian, look at your body and what do you see? A female body. Your body was created to receive a man, just as a man's body was created to enter a woman. This is God's plan through out the universe – positive plus negative, male and female. What is the scientific law we learned in school? 'Like forces repel and unlike forces attract.' To get electricity to work, we have to have a positive and a negative wire...

"I realize you and Celia are thoroughly disillusioned with

124

men, but what kind of men were they? There are good, gentle, kind men, but maybe you looked for them in the wrong places. Are you really happy with yourself? Be honest, and if you really want to change, pray hard and God will help you and also aid you to find a good man to love and care for you. You *can* overcome this problem.

"Then in planning to marry a woman of great emotional instability, who is in and out of the mental hospital and gets these fits of anger (which bring in more D.E.s), have you any idea what you are letting yourself in for? Do you really want to put up with this and why do you want to make it legal? I feel you are not being honest with yourself but are influenced by very destructive forces.

We never heard from Marian again.

This is our feeling about homosexuality and we do not expect all of our readers to agree. There are many facets to consider, but for the most part we feel it can be corrected. Our heart goes out in compassion to those who are attracted to the same sex. They realize it is a deviation from the norm, and since they think there's something wrong with them that cannot be helped, they usually fall into the "gay" or "lesbian" syndrome, meeting with other homosexuals and frequenting gay bars. These are the only places gays can safely congregate, we are told.

It is our opinion that most gays and lesbians are not naturally so but through unfortunate childhood or teenage experiences, have been taught to become so. Boys' schools, we understand, are hot beds of homosexual activity although most of them later change, marry and lead normal lives.

However, there are those who feel strongly inside that they are of the opposite sex and have many of those characteristics. This can be caused by a too-sudden change of sex from that of a past life. For instance, if one had been a woman for several lives and then for karmic reasons, it was necessary to experience life as a male, he could find himself still feeling like a woman inside, with a woman's desire for a man! Usually, souls are prepared over a long period on the inner planes for a sexual changeover but occasionally they come into birth without the necessary preparation. Then too, we find many homosexuals who have brought in these habits from a past life when this way of life was practiced. We know of one man who was a homosexual in several lifetimes and brought this propensity in with him. He now understands this and is beginning to overcome and change his feelings about himself.

We were asked if homosexuality is a situation that should be corrected and does it hinder spiritual growth? We gave a yes to both questions. Let's take it first from the scientific angle – no good or bad connection. One of the first laws we learned in science in school was, "Like forces repel; unlike forces attract." To get electricity to work, we have to have a positive wire and a negative wire. Put two positives or two negatives together and what happens? Nothing. Or it shorts out. We read in an article one time that in homosexual contact over a period of time, the bodies are actually shorted out or burned out. If the records were available, we are sure it would prove that they die much earlier than the average heterosexual person.

In addition, it is contrary to nature's or God's law. The law of our planet and the whole solar system is positive plus negative, male and female – from the tiniest electrons and protons, through mineral, vegetable, and animal kingdoms (although there are some androgynous or self-pollinating plants) so this is broadly stated. It is said that even the planets and stars carry a male or female designation. It is only the human species that consciously thwart this law and practice abnormal perversions.

History proves that the fall of every great civilization was preceded by great sexual degradation, promiscuity, and homosexuality. How people can practice these things and expect to make progress spiritually, we do not know. We are not condemning – only stating facts. Let's look at the reasons.

Many metaphysical books say it is because of a too rapid change of sex when reincarnating, which we previously mentioned.

However, we are finding out that many traumas and sexual problems arise from a child having slept in his parents' room when young. From a book, *The Auric Mirror* we quote:

"A child's unconscious is open and receptive when it sleeps, and on the unconscious level knows all of the activities taking place in a room... It often happens that a child will pretend to be asleep when he isn't. When this happens, the child does not have the emotional and mental maturity to handle the information he has thus received nor does he have the inclination to discuss his feelings. And so all the fear and apprehension become 'locked' in and will emerge in unsuspected behavior and emotional problems."[11]

Then there is another kind, what we call the "neutron" in the electron-proton category. This is a soul who comes in with the knowledge that sex is not necessary in its life. He or she has little or no sexual desire, having previously overcome it, and usually comes into this life to transmute the great creative energy of sex into the higher creativity of lofty music, art, or writing. These are the ones who are "natural" priests or nuns, natural celibates who do not have to be trained in subjugating the sexual desire.

In The Aquarian Gospel by Levi, Jesus described a true "neutron".

"A eunuch is a man who does not lust; some men are eunuchs born, some men are eunuchs by the power of man (castrated), and some are eunuchs by the Holy Breath, who makes them free in God through Christ... He who is able to receive the truth I speak, let him receive." Chapter 143:44[12]

We believe if a person truly wants to overcome his homosexual feelings and practice, he can with God's help. But he must ask for this help by praying from the *heart*, not just mouthing words. He must really want to change and he must pray continuously until he gets results.

Taylor Caldwell, in her wonderful book, *Glory and the Lightning* comments as follows:

"If love between men, of the same sex, were confined to argument and ideas and conversations and the excitement of the exchange of theories, none would have objection... But when men substitute other men in the physical capacity of a woman, then they enter into a twilight world not only of perversion of nature, but in the perversion of their own minds and souls.

"The love between a man and a woman, if really love, is a great mystery and a great glory. It exalts, it edifies, it elevates, it makes them one flesh, almost immune to outward calamity, steadfast, the deepest intimacy any human being can know, beyond friendship, beyond the mere breeding of children."

Tom wrote to us asking to be checked for an entity or entities that were draining him through entertaining sexual thoughts in his mind and other ways. He added that he had formerly attended bars and had had drug experiences so felt he was a prime candidate for D.E.s. He informed us that Spirit had been working with him for the past year and he had quit drinking, smoking, and going to bars. However, the sex desires wouldn't go.

He wrote, "I have reason to believe that someone is impinging on my aura and draining me for I should not have this insatiable desire for sex – morning, noon, and night." (These were homosexual desires, he told us later.) He said this had started when he was about eight years old.

We found a very deep infiltration of many D.E.s with him, inside and outside the aura as well as a partial possession inside the physical body. His High Self was completely blocked as were any spiritual guides. The psychic door was open and there were eighteen D.E.s in the home. A release was completed for him.

Tom replied: "Last night there must have been a release for tonight I feel free. The homosexual demons that were plaguing me have gone for now and I hope they don't come back... I am working with the affirmations you sent me. God bless you.

"I'm anxious for this new experience with women and to live with my upcoming wife and enjoy healthy sexual relations and not unhealthy sex with a man. All these years I have been robbed from being whole and have suffered greatly."

A few days later Tom wrote that something had entered his aura. He said that it came through his left side and took place at work. Another release was done, but the aura was still damaged, especially on the left side. We found that his psychic door was open and this was closed, with a new doorkeeper assigned. Interestingly, his second chakra was damaged and this was the area where the possessing entity had been attached.

The next month Tom wrote that "an entity has entered (now they're trying to get in on the right side) and the 'homo' thing is working on me. I feel inner stress becoming very high. All it wants is to gratify its sexual desires. And all I want is to be the God-individual I really am." He added, "The entities get in at work (smoke-filled room). I am a highly sensitive being and I know when an entity comes upon me." We remind the reader that the aura had not completely healed so he was doubly vulnerable.

We found more D.E.s attached outside the aura and a release was accomplished. Also we sent him the sheet on building the Sacred Inner Shrine (see Chapter 15, Protection and Pitfalls) and more instructions on how to protect himself. However, he wrote once a month for the next four months, but after each release, there were fewer D.E.s the next time. He wrote that his faculties had been opened up so that he knew when the D.E.s entered – that he received certain signals and indications.

As an added protection, we asked for two astral guards, (American Indian) to stay with him and these were assigned. Tom also said that he was diligently practicing the program of building the inner shrine, but he was still having trouble from time to time with the old sexual desires.

Then we received a letter from Tom telling us that he had gone to another state to visit a foundation dedicated to the release of entities. He said, "Their finding was that I had a deep rooted possession named Donald Brook who was a raving sex maniac." The staff of five went right to work on him and finally got him loose and sent on into the light. Gratefully, he added, "In combining your beautiful work and Bettie's (this group is no longer active), I am a free spirit in Christ and I'm so happy, Aloa. Now I have this business of changing the memory track and computer bank and I shall use your exercise of changing the energy pattern."

We rejoiced with Tom that he was now completely free, but we were also chagrined that we had not discovered that entity! We prayed fervently asking our spiritual teachers why we had been told he was clear? Finally we received the answer that he had been hiding in the aura and even They did not know he was there. This was no doubt the original possessing entity that had been pushed out of the physical body into the aura during our release. Tom confirmed that he wanted to keep satisfying the cravings and passions of his sexual energy.

We remembered that we had been warned of this while in training that it was possible for an entity to hide in the aura for a period after a release. We find that the lines of force which are an integral part of the aura become distorted to a great or moderate degree, depending on the depth and type of invasion. This confusion in the aura is due to the intensity of the spiritual cleansing forces and it takes time for these lines to reorient themselves. It is very rare, but possible for a clever D.E. to hide in this confusion for a period and remain undetected. Tom has kept in contact with us for a period of four years and his devotional practices have strengthened his aura to the point that for several years there have been no D.E. attachments. At one time there were satanic forces attacking him from which he was freed and we cautioned him that there was still residue in his aura from the old patterns. He told us that he was beginning to do spiritual work in helping others and we felt that he was opening himself up too much in his zeal – that he must be more impersonal in his work and not take on the emotions and problems of his clients, as well as to protect himself more adequately.

We have had many joyous, heart-warming letters from Tom as he has grown in the light, completely overcoming the sex addiction and enjoying his work in a small church. Not long ago he wrote again for help, but there were no D.E.s. We found an elemental attachment on his emotional body which was removed, and he has been clear since. He is serving in a dedicated healing group as well as working in certain phases of the light work by doing consultation.

Tom's case, and others similar to it, prove that homosexuality can be overcome if one is willing to work and change himself.

CHAPTER 14

Walk-ins

The subject of walk-ins is very popular, especially since Ruth Montgomery has written two books about them, *Strangers Among Us* and *Aliens Among Us*. However, she claims they are coming in at the rate of thousands per day, and we do question this number. A very prominent exponent of the Alice Bailey teachings said recently that there is no such thing as a walk-in, that they are all *possessions*. That is extreme and we cannot agree with that either.

A walk-in, according to our understanding, is a highly evolved being who has a mission to perform on earth and cannot take the time for a baby body to grow to adulthood. He feels he must come in *now* and so receives permission from the karmic hoard. A suitable body is chosen and arrangements are made with the soul and its karmic pattern. That soul agrees to leave its physical body and go on, as in death, and extra "points" are given this soul for donating its body for a high purpose. Then, usually through an accident or serious illness, this soul leaves the body which is immediately entered by the new "walk-in".

People have written us that they have had several walk-ins; some say they have had as many as eight or nine "temporary"walk-ins who come in to help the person during a traumatic crisis and then bow out again!

This is not possible. First, there is the problem of the "silver cord", which is and must be broken when the original soul goes on. We are told that only a high Master or initiate, as Jesus is, can re-attach a new silver cord for the incoming walk-in —when it is for a special mission.

131

Because this is quite common now does not mean that other beings come in and out again just to help us over some rough spots or stand by to come in and help! This is the work of our spiritual guides — and they *never* enter an aura or a body. *This is against Cosmic law.* If one did, it would be just as bad as an earthbound entity possession.

We certainly do not have all the answers on walk-ins, but we do feel within ourselves that the original soul and personality components as a rule leave completely, just as through death, and the silver cord is broken so that the higher being can use the body. He must have his own astral or emotional, mental, and higher bodies, and also must have his own silver cord attached by an initiate.

Several people who claimed to be or have had walk-ins said their astrology charts were still working, others said theirs were not. We felt that people who find their charts still working are possessed, or the walk-in might be another aspect of their own consciousness.

It is important to be ever-discerning and not gullible. There is always a personality change when there has been a true walk-in and often a memory loss or failure to recognize old friends.

In the book, *The Night Has a Thousand Saucers*[14] by Calvin Girvin — an early walk-in from World War II — a space man took over Calvin's body. He tells of overshadowing Calvin for a period of time to learn his habits and also went to his home and tried to become familiar with family and friends (while invisible). He gave this in a lecture we heard, so it may not all be in the book. But his body was shot up so badly, medically they thought he was dead. The "new" Calvin, who had entered the body, applied certain ointments he had, and in three days the wounds were all healed, leaving strange white spots in their place. When Calvin was sent home, his personality was so changed, his family attributed it to the shock. This makes sense to us.

A spiritual teacher, Nathant, who is also a representative of the Great White Brotherhood, explained the walk-in process in a channeled message given on October 19, 1962. This was before the term "walk-in" had been coined. We will quote in part:

"I would say to you then that there are two means by which (a higher being) can take up a given mission in an earthly body.

One would be to create such a body according to that which he would wish to accomplish. However, this is accomplished only when an earthly physical body is not available... Often times several have had the use of an earthly physical body. Many times this is accomplished at a time of crisis in the physical body. You understand, of course, that when this is done, the original spirit of the body agrees to the transfer of awareness, and then returns from whence it came. This leaves the body which can then be utilized at a great saving of time on our part. Not only that, but we have a ready-made condition in which to operate, and environment that is sometimes vitally necessary for our work.

We cannot, of course, ever interfere, nor would we desire to, with the free will of that entity and spirit which originally inhabited that earthly body. To accomplish such an exchange, we must take possession within a maximum of thirty of your minutes, as no longer time span is allotted for the transfer of the spirit and awareness. You understand that our sole purpose in making such an exchange of awareness in an earthly physical body is to expedite our work and our help, born out of love and love only, for the higher progression of awareness within mankind.

A body experiencing physical crisis (such as severe illness) when the exchange is made often recovers completely, but contains a new personality that is often noted by those attending the body. The new awareness within the body is made aware of the body's memory patterns, which permits the new awareness to have recollection of the former physical activity and environment, and therefore life can, for the most part, be resumed with the recovery of the physical body."

We must mention here the Yoga Siddhis – the ability to enter another's body "at will". This is done with permission of the owner of the body in order to permit the yogi to do his work remotely.[15] But a yogi has been trained for many years to do this and knows how to temporarily use another's body without harming it. We do not believe anyone in the west is trained to do this safely.

The above explanations would point out the probability that this procedure could not be such a common occurrence that "thousands" of walk-ins are taking over bodies each day!

We also wish to emphasize the probability that in most cases, the walk-in is a possession by a discarnate entity. This can also take place during a severe illness with a resulting personality change.

CHAPTER 15

Protection And Pitfalls

The importance of protecting one's self from the forces of evil that surround us constantly cannot be stressed strongly enough. To take this for granted is absurd and is akin to neglecting to lock up the house at night or when one is away, just supposing all will be protected! We have to do our part, which means everything possible, including calling to the angels and Beings of Light and asking for protection. They do not do this automatically —we have to *ask*.

A woman we knew who was loaded with D.E.s to the point of insanity, when confronted with this information, said, "Oh, I know I'm protected. God always protects me"

We replied, "But you are not protected unless you ask and use the light consciously to surround yourself."

She believed herself to be the Virgin Mary, and had left her husband and children to attach herself to a man who claimed he was Jesus! We were unable to do anything for them as they did not wish to be helped.

The electromagnetic field around the body, called the aura, is a natural protector when the body is strong and healthy, and one's emotions are under control. Unfortunately, very few people are in this category and even they are subject to an occasional weakening or opening of the auric shield through illness and accident, or display of intense anger, despondency or worry.

There are many methods of protection and we will pass on a few of them to you. Any method of protection should be used in the morning before you leave the house and at night before going

135

to sleep. It should also be used at other times of danger such as going into a bar, a cemetery, or any place of low vibration.

We prefer the following: Ask for, and with the power of the mind, visualize a circle and tube of blazing white Christ Light around the outside of the aura and underneath the feet, about three feet out from the body. The top of this tube will blend with the great White Light coming from the High Self. Then call for a "mirror-like substance all around the outside so that anything of a negative nature that tries to touch it will be immediately reflected back to its source, and we send it back with Divine Love". Returning it with love is important. The evil ones don't mind their energy coming back – they just use it over. But when it comes with Divine Love, they cannot use it unless they turn to the Light. Now fill all the space inside the aura with Divine, Impersonal Love. Feel it filling your heart and Being, then expanding out to fill the whole aura.

For very special or extra protection, you may use the following in addition to the Tube of Light. Visualize a double shield of violet light in front and back of the physical body, from the shoulders to the feet. Then place over your head a golden helmet with visor and golden mesh down to the shoulders and golden boots on your feet. Complete it by using the Tube of Light as above.

This is an armor for protection only and has nothing to do with fighting or doing battle, and the shields are a symbol of God's protecting care. The Apostle Paul says, "Put on the whole armor of God, that ye may be able to stand against the wiles of the devil... Wherefore take unto you the whole armor of God that ye may be able to withstand in the end day... Stand therefore, having your loins girt about with truth and having on the breastplate of righteousness. And your feet shod with the preparation of the gospel of peace. Above all, taking the shield of faith wherewith ye shall be able to quench all the fiery darts of the wicked. And take the helmet of salvation and the sword of the spirit, which is the word of God." Ephesians 6:11-17.

We highly recommend the Prayer of Protection from the Unity School of Christianity:

The Light of God surrounds me;
The love of God enfolds me;
The power of God protects me;
The presence of God watches over me;
Wherever I am God is!

Another very powerful exercise may be done in conjunction with the tube of white Light or any time. Breathe in from the top of the head where the Christ light comes in, all the way down to the toes. While breathing in, silently say, "Father, I breathe in Thy holy breath." Then breathe it out through the space below the feet, saying: "And I breathe out the pattern of sin, sickness, old age and death." Breathe through the nose always and take three breaths in all. We give credit to the beloved teacher, Inis Irene Hurd for this prayer.

Warnings are in order at this time regarding certain seemingly innocuous practices that are being performed by many people without adequate protection. Meditation is one. Never go into meditation alone or in a group (especially in a group) without putting yourself in protection. The dark forces are just waiting for a chance to attack those in the light and we must be wise and alert.

One well-known group has a technique they use for "cleansing the aura". A friend allowed it to be done and said she got a horrible feeling that they had opened her aura, with no closing afterward. It begins with pulling the fingers through the aura from the forehead back over the head – then in the neck area, over and over until the client feels cleansed, tingly, or has chills. A doctor told us he had the same feeling about it –that it is not cleansing, just changing the vibrations and leaving the aura open.

At a spiritual retreat the writer and a friend attended, we were told of another method of "cleansing the aura" and were invited to participate. We stood between two people, one of whom made a cutting motion down the front to "open the aura", then they both proceeded to make great sweeping motions over the body to flush out any debris or negative energy. The aura was not closed afterward either; neither was protection used beforehand. The next morning we were so drained of energy, neither one of us could get out of bed. We were horrified and wondered what could have happened to us! I was especially concerned because I had to give a lecture in a few hours.

Suddenly the thought occurred to us that our auras had been invaded by D.E.s the day before. Ellen and I had just been trained in release work but were very new at it. We got our pendulums and checked each other out. Sure enough, we each had some D.E.s outside the aura. We did a release together, and in minutes the energy began to flow back into our bodies and we felt strong and alert, grateful to have had the experience so we could be aware and warn others.

In any kind of practice where the aura is involved, both the participant and the practitioner must be placed in protective light, also one should call on the guardian angels for their protection. Then the room should be cleansed of any discarnate forces lurking about, and finally, after the work is completed, the aura must be *closed*. This should be done with circular, clockwise movements with a statement to the effect that the aura is being closed and sealed in the white light of the Christ.

If you are in a place where there is a feeling of darkness or fear, besides using the protective light, fold your arms over your solar plexus and repeat the Twenty-Third Psalm over and over – silently, if in a group.

A young woman was alone in the house with her baby girl – her husband was in the Navy. One night she felt strange, fearsome forces around her and could not sleep but kept getting more and more frightened. Finally, she arose and got the baby out of her crib in the next room and took her to bed for comfort. Then she began to repeat the Twenty-Third Psalm over and over. Soon all the feelings of fear and apprehension left and she fell asleep.

Our former president, Franklin D. Roosevelt, said during World War II that "There is nothing to fear but fear itself". Someone else has said that fear is the "real devil", and we would add that the greatest pitfall of all, on our path of life, is *fear*. It is fear of the unknown that blocks man's progress, fear of people or what people will say that grinds him down; fear of the devil and hell keeps him tied to binding religious beliefs, and a thousand other fears – nameless fears that paralyze clear positive thinking and noble aims.

Long ago, leaders found that people could be easily controlled through fear. False priesthoods became established, teaching religions based on fear – of devils, of punishment, and of *God!* The concept of a thundering, wrathful, jealous God as depicted in the Old Testament is a far cry from the loving Heavenly-Father principle that Jesus Christ taught us. The disciple John said, "Perfect love casteth out fear", 1 John 4:18, and Jesus himself said, "Let not your heart be troubled, neither let it be afraid." John 14:27.

Fear of demons, devils, witchcraft, or the black arts is just what it takes to weaken one's energy field and open one's self to possible psychic attack or attachment by D.E.s. We were told in a lecture one time to "laugh at the devil or anything of a demonic nature". The dark forces cannot stand to be laughed at, and laughing takes away all traces of fear. Can you be afraid of something while you are laughing? Laugh inwardly or outwardly, it doesn't matter. They cannot harm you when your trust is firmly in God and you have no *fear.*

We have had very few requests where a specific fear is named, but the following case is one illustration:

When Patrick's mother wrote asking us to do a release for him, she did not mention any specific problem. We found eleven D.E.s inside and outside the aura. Also, his self evaluation, willpower, and determination were all below average. After the release, she wrote to thank us and commented: "Patrick is thirty-two years old and is looking for fulfilling work that pays a wage he can live on. Your work is helping him release fears of black people. We have lived with black people all of our lives and his projection of fear of them, which is so irrational, is being eliminated."

The Apostle Paul tells us: "Put on the whole armor of God, that ye may be able to stand against principalities, against powers, against the rulers of the darkness of this world, against spiritual wickedness in high places. Wherefore take unto you the whole armor of God, that ye may be able to withstand in the evil day, and having done all, to stand. Stand therefore, having your loins girt about with truth, and having on the breastplate of righteousness; and your feet shod with the preparation of the gospel of peace;

Above all, taking the shield of faith, wherewith ye shall be able to quench all the fiery darts of the wicked. And take the helmet of salvation, and the sword of the Spirit, which is the word of God." Eph. 6:11-17.

On the following page you will find a Light Meditation described. This is not something that will appeal to everyone, but those who desire to faithfully practice this procedure will find great spiritual benefit. It will cleanse and protect the four lower bodies as well as balance the heart and crown centers (or chakras) with the Higher Self. Although the throat and brow centers are not mentioned, they will also receive the balancing treatment.

LIGHT MEDITATION TO BUILD THE INNER SHRINE

Sit in chair with feet flat on floor, back straight, hands held out about twelve inches away, palms facing heart center so energy will go towards self. Then visualize a Violet Flame sweeping up through the feet, swirling through the lower bodies and bathing every cell with its cleansing, transmuting power. This is a cleansing process to remove cloudiness or darkness and build the Inner Shrine. We should do this every day in order to become a pure channel for the Christ Light.

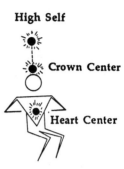

High Self

Crown Center

Heart Center

- Now think of the High Self as a sun and visualize a Golden Light coming from this sun — like a star or flame over your head — and entering through the top of the head.
- When the Light is steady and is seen with the "inner eye" or felt, go to the Heart Center and visualize the sparkling star as before. Now extend the Light by thought until you feel the energy flow slowly through your body down to the feet. You may feel a tingle or warmth.
- Now bring the Light back up to the heart and expand it out to the Etheric Body, then the Astral or Emotional Body, then to the Mental — illuminating every atom.
- After cleansing and balancing the above bodies by use of the Christ Energy which flows into your crown and through your hands, fill your entire being with sparkling Blue-White Light

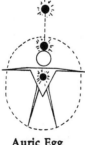

Auric Egg

This same Light will also be used to encircle your magnetic field which is egg-shaped (like the field that encircles the earth). This will protect you from mass consciousness and evil thoughts directed toward you. The opening at the top will direct the Christ Light to you and protect you from all darkness. You are in Reality a small universe in orbit — a '*star*' becoming:

CHAPTER 16

Forgiveness

Forgiveness is of the utmost importance, not only to be able to forgive others but also to forgive ourselves – and this is often the most difficult. It is important that we take time to go back into the memory bank, even to childhood, and as naughty things we did come to mind (it may even bring guilt or humiliation to think of them) we must forgive. Every unkind thing we have done or said to another or that they have done to us, must be forgiven and replaced with love. The sooner we ask another's forgiveness for something we have said or done to them, the easier it is! If we had trouble with one or both of our parents, we must learn to forgive them, realizing that even in their misunderstanding and often seeming cruelty to us, they were doing what they thought was best.

After a release has been completed, it is important to forgive the negative personalities that had attached themselves to you. These entities may or may not have come in willingly, but in forgiving them, you free yourself from the old patterns and thoughtforms they left with you. Forgiveness clears the subconscious mind from old guilt patterns that have long been buried.

Then it is of equal importance to *be* forgiven – to ask God, our heavenly Father, to forgive us for wrong deeds and thoughts. To feel God's loving forgiveness is a release from guilt and removes all the burdens of previous wrong-doing. Jesus Christ made some very pertinent statements about forgiveness and we shall quote several in this chapter. He said, "For if ye forgive men their trespasses, your heavenly Father will also forgive you." Mt. 6:14.

142

When Jesus was hanging on the cross, he prayed, "Father, forgive them for they know not what they do." Lk. 23:34. And in his first Epistle, John says: "If we confess our sins, he is faithful and just to forgive us our sins, and to cleanse us from all unrighteousness." 1 Jn. 1:9

How difficult it often is to love one's self. One's own guilt looms like an impenetrable wall around him, often blocking his ability to accept love from others because he feels he does not deserve it. So in imagination, take yourself tenderly in your arms and say," I love you and God loves you. Of course, you have made mistakes and even sinned, but this was all part of learning and growing and I love you and forgive you."

Here is a wonderful Unity prayer or affirmation that is very helpful:

I forgive others and I forgive myself. God forgives me and I am free.

Say this over and over, from your heart, until you really feel free and guilt is gone. This may take several days, and when other things come to mind that need forgiving, repeat the process. And from now on when something occurs that needs forgiveness, try to forgive immediately. On-the-spot forgiving requires an impersonal attitude, in other words, a refusal to be hurt. Think, "I am God's child, a part of God, and no one can hurt God so they can't hurt me either!" This takes practice to accomplish, but you will find that you can rise above hurts and mistakes with God's help.

Remember that God does not condemn us, we condemn and punish ourselves. Our Father-Mother, Divine Principle, is *all love* and waits patiently for us to stop torturing ourselves with negative emotions and immerse ourselves in His love. Jesus Christ showed us the way, and when Peter asked how many times one should forgive his brother – till seven times? Jesus answered, "I say not unto thee until seven times: but, until seventy times seven".Matt. 18:21

Not only must people be taught to forgive themselves and others, but it is necessary for them to clean out their own garbage; they must learn to transmute and return their own negativity to its source. After forgiving himself and others and accepting God's

forgiveness, one should make use of the *violet transmuting flame.*
We are responsible for our own negative debris, even though it was
left by the D.E.s, but it can be dissolved and transmuted by using
the violet flame, visualizing it sweeping through each of the four
lower bodies: mental, emotional, etheric, and physical. This
should be followed by filling each body with *golden light.*

The above method should also be used for helping the earth
to hold a balance. This is a great service – to cleanse and
transmute for the earth the negativity that man has placed upon
her. It is also very important in group work and a world traveler
and lecturer gave us the following instruction:

"Whenever people gather in a group, they must first protect
themselves by invoking the protective white light of the Christ and
affirming that they will accept no energy that does not come
directly through their Christ consciousness.

"Secondly, that when they have finished their meeting, they
will take the extra energy built up there and use it to release from
the earth any negativity in the area, beginning with their own.
Cleanse it with the violet flame and transmute it into light, sending
it back to its source. The negativity must be dispersed from the
earth plane so the earth does not have to take on the burden of
man's negative energy.

"When they become attuned to the earth consciousness and
not only release, but neutralize the negative energy and return it to
the light, the God consciousness can then carry the transmuted
energy forward and use it in the positive way it was meant to be
used."

We trust every reader will try to participate in this.

A book has been published recently which we feel is the best
self-help book available and we highly recommend it. It is *"Cutting
the Ties That Bind"* by Phyllis Krystal (See Bibliography) and will
certainly aid in clearing the debris left by D.E.s as well as trauma
from childhood and other past experiences.

Now, let us remember that we should make it our goal to love
as God loves and let Him live and express through us. Of course,
a spark of God is in everyone, but it is the conscious awareness and
acceptance that makes it work. It is not an easy path and we may
slip often, but always He is waiting to welcome us back in love and
forgiveness. But don't think this path is a grim, hard struggle. It is

not! The more we surrender our life, our desires, and our will to God's Will, the easier and more joyous life becomes, and we can attest to this. Keeping a joyous attitude is a great goal. It is we who put blocks in our way which cut us off from the feelings of joy and love, which are GOD.

CHAPTER 17

Physical Problems

Everyone who receives a release is helped to a degree — to the degree that their problems were caused by the discarnate entities. Sometimes we find that a possessing D.E. had died of a specific illness which had been passed on to the person whose body he was using. In that case, after the release, there is usually a complete remission or healing of the disease. But in cases of birth injuries and defects or brain damage from an accident, we find that there will not be as much change, although there can be some improvement with a feeling of less stress and better sleeping habits. However, in every case of this kind that we have had, there was either a partial or complete possession at the time of birth or later, through an accident. Consequently, after a release, the changes in personality are always obvious.

Peggy was a beautiful young lady, aged thirty-three, who was almost totally deaf. Her birth had been long and difficult and finally a Caesarean was done. She was born completely deaf in one ear with an 85% loss in the other. Her mother had taught her to speak, but she had been given little education.

The German grandmother who lived in the home was a good woman but extremely domineering. Her father was such a severe alcoholic that her mother left him when Peggy was quite young, but she had had a miserable childhood with her mother and the almost tyrannical grandmother. At age twelve, Peggy tripped over a coffee table that had a spike which punctured her forehead, leaving her unconscious with severe bleeding. About this time, they heard of the death of her father.

Soon after, the girl began to have strange spells of screaming and uncontrolled behavior. She later married, but the husband was so cruel she was afraid of him, so she divorced him. Finally the spells were so severe that she was admitted to a state hospital, but then the mother took her to court and had her discharged. She worked with Peggy mostly alone, although she was seeing a psychiatrist who was unable to help her. We were sent Peggy's picture along with a request for help. In the analysis we found a very deep infiltration of twenty-seven D.E.s, including a partial possession. Five had entered at birth, and the others during the accident. Interestingly enough, Peggy's father, who had died shortly before the accident, was one of the D.E.s attached outside her aura. But none of them were deaf or had caused the deafness. Also, Peggy's High Self was completely blocked and she had no spiritual guides. Her psychic door at the base of the skull was open also, and we found twenty-two D.E.s in the home. A release was completed for Peggy, the psychic door closed, and her home was cleared. A restoration period of three to four months was suggested.

A few months later we received a letter stating that Peggy had been so much improved that she and her mother had gone on a vacation, but stayed in a motel where two men were smoking marijuana next door and they could smell it. Later they moved into a building where marijuana was being smoked and the smell wafted down to their apartment. Then Peggy began to have silly spells, giggling out loud in church during Communion and also during a violin solo. We were requested to do a recheck. This time we found twelve D.E.s outside the aura, but there were thirty-eight in that apartment! Peggy's aura had not completely healed yet and although she had not smoked marijuana, the fumes had drawn D.E.s to the building and some had attached to her. Another release ritual was done for Peggy.

What a wonderful response we received! Three months later her friend wrote: "Peggy is doing fine since the second release. She is having acupuncture (treatments) to try to improve her hearing, and is taking dancing lessons, swimming, and trying to loosen her mother's strong tie to her. You did so much for her. Thank you for everything."

✧ ✧ ✧

George was a young man of thirty-three when a friend sent us a request to do a release for him, saying that she wanted to do everything in her power to help him. He had had many accidents and injuries to the body and head and his medical record was practically unknown. His mental condition was as bad as his spiritual condition, both of which indicated a very disturbed situation. He had no home but moved from one place to another, and at that time was living in a hotel.

The release for George was done on a Sunday afternoon and completed by 6:20 pm. (8:20 E.S.T. which was George's time). It is interesting that he and his friend had agreed to meet at 8:00 pm., just while we were working although they were unaware of it. She wrote that at that time he was very intoxicated as well as on some drugs, and the pulse in his wrist was extremely fast. A man who was with him asked her to take care of George as he had done all he could and was helpless.

George said to her, "Well, I said I would put you in charge. Here I am — some prize!" After several stops they arrived at her house.

She continued, "Upon entering the house, he asked me if I had any chains and a lock. He said he wanted me to fix him a bed on the back porch and chain him to the metal supports as he knew he could not move them. Horrified, I listened and he pleaded. He said the 'pressure' he had complained of earlier was so great he was afraid he could not control it and was obviously terrified at what he might do. I had seen him like this three or four times, but always he left or I left. This time, I listened with misgivings and consented to literally chain him to the headboard of the bed, after his tearing the garage apart for a chain and insisting that I take a heavy lock off one of the gates. All I could think of, through my tears, was, 'God, help me to help him.' But was this the way?

"This proceeded to be the most emotional nightmare I have ever had. He pulled and tore and it was like something in an asylum a hundred years ago. I had taken his knife and belt out of the room and hidden them, also matches, a glass, and a hunting gun that had belonged to my son. I lit a cigarette and held it for him.

"He could not wait to get his wrists chained and told me that

148

he might beg, plead, coax, promise or threaten – please do not give in and undo the lock for at least five days! He said the pressure was getting worse and worse. I asked him to take a Valium just to help him calm down and get control, which he did. But before it took effect he cried, begged, and tried everything to get free. Then he became dazed, though still glassy-eyed, but some of the wildness went out of his eyes. We talked but he was somewhat out of his head.

"I asked him to please remember only one thing from tonight – two words, 'Aloa Starr, a healing star'. I repeated it to him and told him that for some reason he was going to be free – I could feel it – but I didn't know when. I would have to wait until I got a letter to tell me. He was somewhat restless the rest of the night and slept most of the next day. I couldn't leave him chained – I couldn't stand it, and he seemed somewhat tired. In the evening he departed as was his wish."

During the analysis, we found that his High Self was blocked and he had no spiritual guides. There was a very deep infiltration of sixty-two D.E.s, including a Complete Possession. They were affecting him emotionally, mentally, and physically. However, in rechecking him after the release, his conscious and subconscious levels were extremely affected still, showing brain damage due to previous head injuries. This mental retardation was not caused by the D.E.s.

About five days later, a recheck was done. There were five D.E.s outside the aura and another release was completed. The restoration period was to be ninety days, if he would try to help himself and stay off drugs and alcohol.

His friend wrote: "I fully well realize that the drugs and alcohol do not help. I have tried every possible means – legal to psychological – all pretty much to no avail. He is little by little trying to do better and something within wants to, but it is going to be sometime before there is complete change of a deepdown, long-lasting nature. Only he can get these things under control. With your help and that of others who have become interested, maybe we can pull him through this. I will keep in touch as I know we will badly need your assistance."

About six months later, she wrote for another release for George. His High Self was only partly connected and there were nineteen D.E.s outside the aura. We did not get permission from our High Self to do a release for him, as he would only draw more negative D.E.s to himself through his continued use of drugs and alcohol. She wrote that George no longer seemed to be in control after a rather see-saw type of progress. She said, " we are hoping for a forced hospitalization which should last five days, with some possibility of a voluntary commitment from him. We have no idea what the test results will be."

This was the last word that we received.

Phyllis wrote that seven years before writing us, she had begun to attend a spiritualistic group, who discovered that she was very sensitive and "opened up" quickly. Her first experience of hearing" voices and seeing pictures" were happy and beautiful, and a particular Voice took her back through previous lifetimes. Then this voice and others began to take control of her and she began to give "readings". Then feelings of harassment began to develop and she began to lose control of herself. Phyllis then contacted a psychiatrist and was hospitalized for a month. At that time she was walking like a stiff doll — felt an entity was walking through her! While at the hospital, under medication, she said everything left her and she began to feel completely normal. She took a job as her doctor advised.

She was free for a year and then harassment returned. She saw an entity standing by her bed one night, white and looking like a snowman; with a sense of arrogance about him. It was after this incident that her problems returned in the form of heavy weights and pressure around her head and shoulders; then pain and electric-like vibrations up and down her feet and legs. Often a feeling of something claw-like and sharp being stuck into her occurred but an intensive physical and neurological examination revealed nothing and her psychiatrist said he was unable to help. Also, she experienced a phenomenon of seeing colors and objects in the air. For the next three years she visited various mediums who all recognized a psychic problem but were unable to help her.

The following year, Phyllis had an exorcism by three priests and a nun who was a healer, but this was unsuccessful.

Several months later, after our work in which we found a very deep infiltration of D.E.s, including a Partial Possession, she wrote that the situation had not changed. A recheck was performed which showed that more entities had attached outside the aura only, and they were released. However, we also found that the etheric web, between the etheric and astral bodies, was damaged, leaving it half open. There was also a demonic contact. At this time we received the information that Phyllis had been a high priestess with these dark forces in the distant past. Even though she had been cut free, they were still harassing her. We urged her to denounce these forces herself, in the Name of Jesus Christ, and say emphatically that she would have no more to do with them unless they turned to the Light – that this was the only true way. Also, we suggested that she use eucalyptus oil and Sea Breeze on her person as negative forces find it repulsive. She was also told to work on forgiving these forces, forgiving herself for her past mistakes, and asking God's forgiveness.

After this we heard no more from Phyllis, so could only assume that either she was free or that there were other factors involved which blocked her freedom from these evil forces. They were not earthbound, but appeared to be from the lower astral realm.

✧ ✧ ✧

Dora went into a deep depression about a year after she learned she had cancer. Then she had several fearful experiences, one in which a satanic force seemed to jump off a cross on the highway and sit on the back of the front seat of her car.

It said, "Aha, I've got you now."

She could not sleep because of strange noises in the night. There were large, weird tracks where she went for a walk in the desert, and she would see fearsome faces in everything – like plastered walls, shag carpeting, clouds, etc. She tried to commit suicide twice and her husband and family were very concerned. She also had difficulty conversing with anyone and was afraid to answer the phone or doorbell.

An analysis was done and we found that the High Self was not in contact and there were no spiritual guides. Twenty-one D.E.s were lodged inside and outside the aura, with a Partial Possession inside the physical body. They were affecting her mentally, emotionally, and physically. There was also a supra-physical shell from a past life that was affecting her.

Three days after the first release was completed, and she showed "clear", we found four more D.E.s had attached to the aura which was very badly damaged and evidenced "cracks", apparently from all the drugs she had received.

After the second release, she reported that she had served a dinner for guests, perfectly at ease and had a marvelous time. They entertained three other couples for dinner, and went out to a friend's home since then – all easy and pleasant.

Dora's husband remarked, "Whatever you're doing must be the right thing!"

It was necessary to do two more releases for her, one three weeks later when we found four D.E.s outside the aura. She was told to visualize the violet light on the cracks in her aura and to use the forgiveness affirmation. (See chapter on Forgiveness.) Her High Self was back in good contact and she now had five spiritual guides.

Five months after the first release, she checked out "clear". Her aura was completely healed and the fear was GONE! And she joyfully reported that the *cancer had been arrested*! So, in this case, a physical problem was definitely helped.

❖ ❖ ❖

Mrs. R. wrote concerning her daughter, Jeanie, who had cerebral palsy, adding that she had had brain surgery three weeks before to help loosen her right leg and arm.

"On the day after we returned home", she said, "Jeanie went into a state of shock and was hospitalized. She is home and hopefully recovering now... but I have a feeling possession of a sort is involved. I would like you to clear her."

In doing the analysis, we found a deep infiltration of D.E.s inside and outside the aura, and a possession in the physical. Quite a few had come in at birth, with a few more at the time of the operation, and these had brought on the seizure. Inner stress was extremely high and came down two hundred points after the release! We cautioned Mrs. R. not to expect much change in the cerebral palsy from our work, as we felt the D.E.s had probably not caused it and it seemed to be a karmic condition.

However, she wrote back later: "Thank you for the clearing of my daughter, Jeanie. She is doing beautifully now with no more of the possession or seizure attacks. We thank God for the blessings of this year. Your work has been most meaningful and beautiful for us and many others, I'm sure! God bless you and your work." We were most gratified by the results of this release.

✧ ✧ ✧

Illnesses that are diagnosed as "schizophrenia" and" epilepsy" are almost always caused by the infiltration of discarnate entities such as a Possession or a Partial Possession, or an instrument implant. Even where there has been brain damage causing the epilepsy, there is always the added problem of D.E. attachment. In schizophrenia or "split personality", we feel it is always a D.E. complication, even though there are also problems of the psyche.

The name of Bryan P. was sent to us for release in the fall of 1975. He had been a ward of Mrs. Margot G. for twenty-six years, having come to her at age twenty-two. Bryan's mother had died when he was sixteen, about ten months after he had "the first dreadful experience in the mental hospital". Margot said there was no evidence of an emotional problem before he was fifteen. He had had a sledding accident at age thirteen, which caused structural damage to his mouth, back of head, and upper spine. A severe scoliosis (curvature of the spine) was the result. He had been an honor student at a prestigious boys' academy and was a Junior at fifteen. He was diagnosed schizophrenic and returned to his father, who simply could not communicate or cope with his son. After Margot accepted him, the father kept in touch and continued to pay much of Bryan's expenses.

At the time we began to work with Bryan, he was gradually losing the use of his legs and had difficulty walking, no doubt from the spinal injury. We found a very deep infiltration of D.E.s inside and outside the aura, and a supraphysical shell from a former life. Of course, there were D.E.s in the home as well. His character was not bad, only two points below average and later increased one point. Self evaluation, willpower and determination were all below average but after the release, came up to average. We had no idea then that we would be working with Bryan over a period of ten years, and most of the information we have about him was given in bits and pieces during those years.

Three months later, Margot wrote that a few weeks after the release, she had taken Bryan to a Kathryn Kuhlman healing service. She said, "He was terrified that he might have a healing as he repeated that he was *afraid of life and responsibility*. Two days later he blew up here – struck a guest and we had to have him hospitalized. He has been living in a rehabilitation center but is eager to return home. I am not going to bring him here except on monthly visits. (She did later.) I don't know how much of his problem is attacking entities and how much is a defense against getting well."

She asked us to recheck him and we found five new D.E.s inside and outside the aura and eleven in the home where he was staying. After the release, we gave Margot several methods of protection for Bryan to use to ward off D.E.s and keep himself clear, but he didn't seem interested in helping himself. Also, she said he no longer read books although he was a good reader, and this development made working with him more difficult.

It was several years before we worked with Bryan again and by that time Margot had moved him back to her home and had hired a young man to help her with his care. Bryan was in a wheelchair, having lost the use of his legs while in a mental facility where he was over-drugged and his kidneys damaged.

Then she wrote that it had been necessary to engage another person as the former man had a night job, and this change had been a threat to Bryan. She said, "He was splendid the three weeks before Christmas and until the morning of Christmas Day when he awakened being bombarded by entities and was afraid to get out of bed all day long. Father P. came to give him communion and he was aware of the entities and the power leaving him and going to Bryan, who was much better for about four hours. Then they started to attack again and I added a standing cross and open Bible to the lighted candle, and they left. He had some difficulty yesterday but by Sunday was fine."

We checked Bryan shortly afterwards and found two D.E.s outside the aura, but the room was clear at the time. We felt the attacking entities were a group of low astrals that he may have worked with in the past and advised him to build a shell of Light around himself and we also placed a circle and tube of White Christ Light around him after the release, as we always do. It is important to realize that D.E.s and demons can attack from the outside, even when none are attached.

About six months later, we were asked to check him again. After a very in-depth investigation, we were given some very surprising information – that part of his astral or emotional self was not in his body! The masculine part of him was still in the astral realm and only the feminine part was in his body. According to Dr. Carl Jung, the Swiss psychologist, this would be the "animus" and "anima". This animus part was with the lower astral forces and we felt it wanted to leave them but was afraid of them.

As we worked with the spiritual light and our own inner-plane helpers, the masculine self went willingly with them to a higher temple for training. We advised Bryan to pray for this animus and love it.

Margot wrote back that when she told Bryan about this other part of himself, he did not understand and raged at her, "Did I ever tell you that you were crazy? You're crazy!" So she asked Roger, the aide, to talk to him about this as he could possibly take it better from a male.

Roger had told him in the past, when exercising his legs, "to let his masculinity out". He now talked with him about the masculine part being with the entities and Bryan was able to listen and become thoughtful.

"When I came into his room at three", Margot resumed, "he was sitting waiting for me, a great smile on his face." She said she was impressed to call the other self David, a name in four generations of her family. "Also, Jesus was of the House of David and this made it special." Bryan was quite receptive to the idea and said if David would come back he would forgive him and love and protect him. Then he said, "Let's have a party!"

Margot continued, "He loves champagne which I get occasionally, so we had a party to welcome back David when he was able to come. We called the total "Bryan-David" and had a great deal of fun. After two days of raging and filthy words and a near strike (which disturbed Bryan when he came back to himself), it was a welcome relief...

"Bryan is not the least bit effeminate in appearance or manner although many times he has said he would be better off had he been born a girl and talks often of "Christine Jorgensen", the first sex-change man. He very much wants to be male, is interested in sports, and his ego cannot accept the idea of homosexuality. It would seem to me that he is not immature, but incomplete, which I have long felt, and that the missing part is the creative part. Otherwise, he is a great person who makes you feel good to be around." We felt this indeed confirmed our findings.

A week later, Margot wrote, "Bryan began to improve shortly after I spoke with you and he's still all right. I am so fed up with those entities and feel that they're out to make my life miserable if not kill me. Bryan is fed up with them too, and he couldn't believe it when I said that they could leave him for good. We'll go through any ritual you suggest to help. Bryan loves ritual."

During the next six months, it was necessary to recheck Bryan five times and each time there were from three to twelve D.E.s outside the aura only. He was still somehow attracting them and his damaged aura was letting them in. However, he always seemed better and made more progress after each release.

Finally, Margot wrote some wonderful news just after Christmas. "Bryan is doing splendidly and I do not believe that it would have happened without your help. Since November, he has made steady improvement. This year, twelve of us had Christmas dinner at Father P.'s home and Bryan was a guest. He acted quite at home in the group, looked splendid, and I have never known him to be better. He has done a great deal of free crying for the first time since I have known him, he is able to express appreciation, and now is realizing that he is selfish and has to do something about it."

Several months later, Margot was given some very startling and enlightening information which threw a great deal of light on all Bryan's problems since his teens. She told us, "Bryan has had no problem with D.E.s since you had his psychic door closed last September. I think that we finally have gotten to the bottom of his problem... Father P. gave me a clue after he saw a (T.V.) program on which a woman (spoke) who was seduced by her father. About six weeks ago I realized that the word 'mother' was a threatening word to him and began to refer to him as 'my friend' instead of 'my son'. This week I learned that at the age of fifteen, he had had several sexual experiences with girls while at their summer home at the shore and after he got home, *had intercourse with his mother,* who must have encouraged him. He never had any further experiences with girls, but became mentally disturbed and had the defense

156

mechanism of being homosexual. That was his defense against the material which was buried, *incest!*" This experience, together with the entrance of D.E.s which must have occurred during the sledding accident, we feel, is what triggered the ensuing schizophrenia. Bryan had kept this guilty incident buried and never revealed it through all his years of therapy! As we mentioned, Bryan's mother had died the next year, when he was sixteen.

Later we were told that Bryan was going through a most difficult period. "He just cannot forgive himself, I think, for what happened with his mother", commented Margot. "As a result, he is just bogged down and won't do a thing to help himself. He hates himself and projects this out to the world — hates everyone and is so different from what he was."

Bryan had experienced an operation on his legs several months previously and Margot wrote that it was discouraging for him to have to lie in bed so much. "He listens to classical music by the hour, but I'm afraid his physical condition is hopeless unless he has a spiritual healing. The present two physicians stated that the problem was due to brain damage caused by over-drugging and lack of oxygen to the brain

Apparently the anaesthesia for five and a half hours aggravated the condition and made him more paralyzed. Entities seem to be around him at times, but I can clear his aura and tell them to leave."

Then it was almost Christmas again and Bryan had been back in the hospital for almost three weeks with infected bed sores. We were asked to check and found some D.E.s inside and outside the aura this time, with fifteen in his hospital room. These were released and he went home three days later. He was, by then, totally confined to a wheel chair.

It was sometime later that we heard the surprising news from Margot that Bryan had died. She told us, "He was a wonderful 'old soul' as they called him, and I adored him. He was such a splendid person and had such great vibrations when those negative forces did not plague him. He died last August — not really ill — it all happened in twenty-two hours. He left so gently, my arms around him."

What a beautiful tribute to this man who had suffered so

much. Margot is writing the story of Bryan's life and we were so pleased to have her send us what she said about our work:

"In thirty years of helping a so-called 'incurable schizophrenic', I heard of only one person and her group who could successfully remove these negative forces from the body or aura of an individual. Not only were they removed from the person, but from the earth sphere. Instant or almost instant improvement was observed in each and every person so treated."

We are grateful to have been a part of Bryan's healing and release therapy.

CHAPTER 18

The Healing Ministry Of Release

EXORCISMS ARE REAL, SAYS LADY WHO KNOWS (Ethel DeLoach). These were the headlines from an article in the Atlanta Journal and Constitution, February 10,1974. It went on to say:
"Recently the Archbishop of Canterbury, Michael Ramsey, said there are indeed demonic powers afoot... He went on to say that there are some people with a gift for exorcism, but added, 'It is a very dangerous gift to use. There is danger of the person using it being spiritually damaged. I would not advise it for anybody if they did not have the gift and considerable spiritual depth.'"

To those who feel they would like to do release work, we must point out several prerequisites. First, there must be a definite "calling" and preparation as noted above. Ideally, one should have had at least two or three previous lives in which he had training so that his inner bodies have a certain strength and resistance. This is not a do-it-yourself process, and one must realize the depth of spiritual integrity required of the releasor and the damage or danger involved to the well-meaning, untrained neophyte.

Secondly, there should be harmony in the home and one's mate should be willing to help, at least in the release ritual. To have the added energy is important, and that of a dedicated small group even better. Jesus said, "Where two or three are gathered together, in my name, there am I in the midst of them." Matt. 18:20.

However, if one is single but dedicated, permission can still be given. At first the author was trained with another woman who dropped out after a short while as she was having so many psychic attacks, she felt it was just not her work. So we petitioned the

Father for an inner-plane partner, one who could provide the extra energy and protection required, and this was granted. We called on him every time a release was done and were very much aware of his presence. At times, with the inner eye, we could visualize him at his desk, working right along with us on another plane of consciousness. Also, we have a small, dedicated service group which helps in the release of some of the more difficult cases. And more recently, Spirit brought into our life a wonderful, devoted mate.

Thirdly, this work should not be done where there are young children in the home as they are too undeveloped and vulnerable. From age seven to fourteen, a child's emotional body is developing; and from age fourteen to twentyone, his mental body is maturing. Since we actually contact and speak to discarnate entities, telling them that God loves them and we are here to help them go to the plane of consciousness where they belong, this could be dangerous to younger children who might pick up some of the entities. We suggest twelve as a minimum age.

It was found in our work that often unattached D.E.s were drawn to the house by the spiritual light and would stay around until a release was done. We finally had to make a request for two Indian spirit helpers to keep a permanent compound outside and hold them in abeyance, not allowing them in the house. Then when we were performing a release, we would call the entities in and the other Indian runners would lead them off. Golden Eagle and White Cloud were the guardians.

Lastly, after the evaluation of the problems of the individual have been determined, a specific procedure of release should be commenced, utilizing the aid of spiritual beings from the non-physical worlds. It is absolutely essential to have inner-plane helpers on several levels of consciousness so the entities can actually see them and be led completely away from the earth level. Otherwise, they are free to attach themselves to the same person or to someone else at the first opportunity; *they should not be allowed to remain earthbound.* There are a few people and groups we know of who are doing exorcism work with varying results. For centuries some Catholic priests have been trained in exorcism and also some members of charismatic churches are "casting out devils". As far as we can determine, they do it through the earth-level frequency of their own determination, or by special rituals of prayer and fasting in the name of Jesus Christ, often covering twelve hours to two or three days. Many do excellent work, but when they do succeed in casting them out, the D.E.s are not sent anywhere but are left earthbound, free to attack someone else!

The shock treatments sometimes given in mental hospitals are another method of exorcism and do drive out the invading D.E.s, but with great pain and agony to the patient as it is the extreme electric shock that jolts the body and expels the D.E.s forcibly.

A great deal of modern psychiatric treatments may, in some cases, be found to have their origins apart from the patient's psyche. Some doctors are beginning to suspect the possibility of discarnate entity invasion. F. Scott Peck, M.D., in his best selling book *People of the Lie*,[16] tells of his work in actually exorcising demonic entities.

We would mention here the pioneering work of Carl A. Wicklund, M.D. and Mrs. Wicklund as related in his book, *30 Years Among the Dead*,[17] in which he tells of his contact with D.E.s and their subsequent release during the early 1900s. This book was long out of print but is again available.

Dr. Wicklund devised a method of using static electricity applied to a patient and could thus dislodge the attached spirit or spirits. His wife, Anna, was a trained psychic intermediary who had a group of invisible helpers she called the Mercy Band, which protected her and would also assist the D.E.s to enter her entranced body and use her voice. Dr. Wicklund would then speak to them, finding out who they were, and finally convincing them that they were dead! After agreeing to leave, the spirit helpers would take them away or sometimes a beloved relative who had died would come to get them.

Both of the Wicklunds worked in this way for thirty years, especially with the so-called insane, who would immediately be restored to a balanced mental condition after the release.

The Wicklunds were pioneers in the field of this type of exorcism where the D.E.s actually spoke through a channel in trance. However, in all these years of work, Mrs. Wicklund suffered no ill effects and this is most unusual. We are told that she was constantly surrounded and protected by the Mercy Band and there were many on the inner planes who were closely supervising this project in which they felt there was a decided breakthrough in the contacting and releasing of these often evil and vicious discarnates.

But we must state unequivocally that this procedure is extremely dangerous and in most cases where someone has tried to emulate Mrs. Wicklund's method, it has ended in disaster. We have heard of several and knew one personally.

A very spiritual and dedicated man in California began to work with discarnate entities by somehow freeing them from his patient and then calling them into himself. He would take them within his own aura and talk to them, finally persuading them to go into the light. Apparently, however, they did not always all leave and he began to build up a whole clan of very evil entities, without his even being aware. But he turned from a kind, gentle, humble man to an arrogant, mean and violent maniac. He became ill and was bedridden and his poor wife was beside herself until a friend of ours, a practical nurse, agreed to take him to her home. She said he yelled and swore at her constantly with foulest language, and if she did not come the minute he rang his bell, he would throw things at her, including the alarm clock! After one week, she sent him back to his wife, and mercifully, he died soon after. My friend had considered him to be her spiritual teacher until that episode.

We were told of this after he died or we would certainly have tried to free him.

A woman exorcist we heard of who worked in a similar manner, later died in a mental institution.

A second woman we knew of was a channel for discarnates in a healing and release group that worked in the Christ Light and had some wonderful results. She went into trance and allowed the discarnates to speak through her, and then a minister and his group would release them and send them on with their Indian spirit helpers. However, after a number of years, this channel also began to go through personality changes and became an angry, domineering and hateful person who finally left the group, which then disbanded. (Strange that no one realized that she had taken on D.E. attachments!)

We wish to impress upon the reader the dangers of wilfully

taking D.E.s into one's aura and that it is entirely unnecessary, now that we find a simple pendulum can be used to gain the necessary information. We contact the Higher Self and guardian angel of the patient and through them, via the pendulum, make the pertinent evaluations and then proceed with the release ritual to free the D.E.s, and our invisible helpers lead them away. This, we feel, is a more advanced and far superior method.

There are bands of American Indians on the higher astral planes who can be called on to take discarnate entities away from the earth. Why Indians? Because, even in physical bodies, they are very close to the spirit world and are trained to work with it. For eight years we worked with a group in California that did release work from time to time. We would call in Lone Wolf and Mighty Waterfall and their hundreds of Indian runners, who could be seen by the clairvoyants in the group, wearing white breech clouts and a white feather in their hair!

An interesting note is that as our own work progressed, we found that often the D.E.s were frightened of these half nude Indians and refused to go with them, and we had to take time to explain that they were our helpers and were harmless. So we asked the runners to please change their mode of dress to something more modern – and the next time they came in wearing white jogging suits and jogging shoes! We had a good laugh.

Recently, after many, many years of work, Lone Wolf and Mighty Waterfall left to go into higher levels of progression and have been replaced by Sun Eagle and Double Rainbow. Recently, they went on also and we now have White Elk and Thunderbolt, of the original group. We send the entities on in love and understanding and speak kindly to them, telling them they are dead and are using someone else's body and that we have come to free them. Then we ask for any relatives available to come in and help free them. They are usually more willing to leave when they can see Grandma or Uncle Joe! However, relatives cannot always be contacted or they won't go with them, so we always need the Indian Helpers to lead them away to the plane to which their soul computes them. There are many, many levels in the lower and higher astral planes and according to the kind of life one has lived on earth, he is computed to a similar environment. Like attracts like! But first they are always commanded to come out in the

Name of Jesus Christ. It is His power that does the actual release.

In cases of a very deep Possession or attachments over a long period of time, we ask if the person needs an "Assignment".This is a positive, high-level being who has lived on earth and knows all our temptations and problems. This Being is assigned to stay with the person as long as needed.

After the process is completed and the person has been found to be clear, the spots where the D.E.s were attached are drained and filled with Violet Light. We ask that the Violet Flame sweep through the aura, dissolving and transmuting the old patterns, habits, and negative memories —as much as possible. (The balance is done during the Restoration Period.) Then the whole Aura is filled and sealed in a circle and tube of golden-white light, as given on page 134. But the seal can still be broken if one continues in his old habits or fails to protect himself properly. Protection is essential, especially before sleep and before leaving the house in the morning.

Say firmly: "I STAND IN THE LIGHT OF GOD'S LOVE. I AM ALWAYS PROTECTED AND MY AURA IS SEALED FROM ANY NEGATIVE FORCE." Be sure to visualize and feel this as you say it. Also, call to your Guardian Angel frequently and thank it.

We found it very interesting when a holistic, clairvoyant doctor asked to observe our work. We asked him in turn to describe the colors he saw while we worked, which he jotted down as follows:

During the analysis, as we tuned in through the photo or handwriting of the requestor, he saw a clear green and felt a studious quality.

Then during the buildup of energy for the release and the call for our invisible helpers, he saw blue and green, then a large expansion of golden yellow as the helpers came in. (We feel them come in as a sudden charge or electric-like impulse.)

During the actual release, a brilliant white and a bright red beam came in. He felt great strength and spiritual energy and there were energy lines moving around and around, very fast. At the words, "Light, Light", the white streamed in.

After we finished, sealing the aura with a golden-white light and filling it with love and energy, he saw a yellow glow full of sparks and glittering with a happy, friendly vibration. This gradually became a soft yellow as the final prayer of thanks was given.

Some D.E.s are quite powerful, having been used to a certain body for a long time and simply refuse to leave. Sometimes the D.E. feels it is really "his" body. We tell them if they do not leave willingly, they will be taken by force and we call in a band known as the In-God-We-Trust angels. These have been seen clairvoyantly as small cherubs, but powerful, carrying nets of golden light into which they forcibly place the D.E.s, pulling a cord at the top, and carrying them off. These D.E.s are taken to a place that is called the "Fifth Sun" where they have to stay until they learn God's law. It is against God's law to attach to or to use another's physical body. Then we always call to Archangel Michael and Mighty Astrea for their angels of the Flaming Blue Sword to stand by with their great power and cut free any D.E.s that need this special help. They lend their energy to the whole ceremony.

After that we call to the mighty Archangel Zadkiel for a band of angels of the Violet Flame. This is a cleansing, dissolving and transmuting flame and is used to dissolve the energy of demons, thoughtforms, hexes and spells, mind controls, and to clear out negative energy in homes and other buildings; as well as to cleanse the aura of the patient. After this is done, the spots or areas are always filled with golden or golden-white light.

For those readers who have been trained in other methods of release, we should like to add a few of our findings which may be important to you. The number one admonition is to protect yourself or selves in the white light of the Christ and to use the double shield and golden helmet as explained in Chapter 15.

Next, we call in any relatives who will help, then the angelic and Indian or other astral helpers, and then build up a strong vortex of energy with prayers, mantras, affirmations and music, if required. Then our inner-plane Helpers can take this earthplane energy and expand it thousands of times with their God-power and use it to release the negative entities, demons, and other energies. In this way the release takes place almost immediately, usually within a half hour or less. Thus, hours and days of prayer and/or fasting are not needed. Jesus Christ did this instantaneously and He still does!

However, sometimes we find that we have not built up

enough energy on this plane so that some of the more stubborn ones are still present when we recheck the next day. Occasionally a D.E. possessing the body will be thrown out but still be attached to the aura, and another release must be done. After a release, we find that the auric field is in a state of confusion and sometimes D.E.s can hide in it and not be observed by the Helpers. So we recheck the next day.

When the person to be released is present, it is important that the releasors do not touch the person or become entangled in his aura. We usually have the person seated and the releasor standing about three feet in front of him, with palms held up facing him. The assistant stands in the same way, about three feet behind. The person in the chair should close his eyes and stay in a prayerful mood, but should not try to help in anyway.

As we mentioned, when the release is complete, it is very important to ask that the spots where the D.E.s were attached be drained and filled with love and energy and that any holes in the aura be healed. However, this healing may take from thirty to ninety or more days so the inner bodies may return to a normal pattern. This is because the D.E.s leave debris, old patterns and habits that must be purged and it takes time, especially if they have been there long. We call this the restoration period, although there is always a definite change or reaction within forty-eight hours after the release or sooner. One may experience severe headache, nausea, or crying spells if the infiltration was deep. If not, there is a wonderful feeling of freedom and joy, of being all together and truly one's self. And usually one finds he is sleeping much better.

Restoration is like reprogramming a computer and is helped by prayers, meditation, and affirmations of a positive nature. The person must be willing to change himself, his thoughts and habits for a release to effect permanent change. If he goes back to his old destructive habits, he will only attract new D.E.s to his aura.

Always, after a release, be sure to wash your hands and wrists to break the vibration, so you are not drained of energy. The releasers should feel joyous and uplifted after the ceremony and in no way drained. If they do, they are not protecting themselves adequately. Also, never perform a release when not feeling well physically — even having a headache or cold. The aura is weak and vibrations lower then and one can easily draw in the surrounding

D.E.s, and the resulting release is not always effective. This has happened to the writer several times until she finally learned the lesson and the work for ten or fifteen people had to be done over! It has been most interesting to us to investigate the release methods and information from other groups. We wish to include here a very appropriate excerpt from Cosmic Awareness Communications[9].

Question: "What attracts these (negative) entities to certain people?"

Answer: "This relates in part to the person being receptive or subjective in their consciousness, where they fear such beings and become obsessed with such thoughts and open themselves up for such invasions... People ever and always wish to think that reality relates to science and imagination relates to illusion or religion or fantasy. Nothing could be further from the truth for imagination is that which builds and creates the reality which people enjoy or despise. Very wise people, realizing this phenomena, have set about to attempt to erase this type of manifestation by simply stating that... it is mere fantasy and does not exist!... This has prevented many of these possessive beings from having energy on which to feed in order to possess people in the physical realm... When people believe in them and send them energy with their obsessions and their focusing and their belief in these (evil) forces, the more energy is directed toward them and the more certain and powerful they become. (Still we must be aware they exist.)

"We suggest that also you let every affirmation (for the release of a discarnate) be accompanied by a physical ritual: This can be clapping the hands after an affirmation, or stamping the foot, or lighting a candle, or falling to your knees and giving thanks to those higher spiritual forces... It matters not what the physical action, but the <u>same</u> action should be used each time after an affirmation (or mantra) so your subconscious accepts it (and its meaning)... It can be as simple as snapping your fingers or as complex as a three-day ritual. It depends on what it takes to convince you that the decree is happening. If you still have doubts, then you should go through longer rituals."

C.A. goes on to say that when one is hounded by forces he does not like, a dog that barks or growls will serve much like a banishing ritual. He also mentions cats and that many witches use

167

cats in order to draw in forces for their deeds. But (cats) need not draw in negative forces, it depends on your motive and the kind of force you wish to draw in. The right cat can keep you surrounded by high spiritual forces, drawing or invoking the higher forces or energies for your purpose. (Note: But one must be very careful in this because some animals are possessed by a negative force or an elemental.) This Awareness continues by saying that none of the above can happen except through the opening or doorway which people create by imagining negative forces attacking them. He says they can attack innocent people but the negative force cannot gain foothold except wherein someone or some force gives them the energy to do so.

To counter a black magician, he advises one to build a shield around himself that will not allow a penetration of these energies. He advises one to visualize the destructive entity striking the shield and reflecting the black magic back upon the magician, but a physical action must accompany the imaging, He also says that in reflecting back the image or energy of the black magician or negative force, the person must feel satisfied and unafraid, must feel confident that the force has not penetrated the shield – the imagined shield – and when one *feels* this, there can be no penetration. He says if one is simply "hoping" the shield will withhold the attack, then he is working with a very thin protective device.

To strengthen the shield, one must repeat the imagery process again and again until satisfied, or create physical actions or rituals which reinforce the imagery process. Then he adds that instead of just bouncing back the negative energy, one may wish to transmute that force into white light with the idea that you will change this evil energy and turn it into light and this light shall return to the black magician and destroy the darkness and light up the entity toward higher divine purposes. This is much more damaging to the black magician than to simply throw back his energy for they do not mind their energy coming back to them as much as having transmuted energy coming back to change their entire being into light – such entities actually fear light. This Awareness suggests that this is the most appropriate method to deal with dark forces of this type.

He adds that one may visualize wrapping that dark force

168

with the law of love and chaining or binding it with the law-of-love symbol (this is two concentric circles), "binding the dark force like a cocoon of clear white light, completely enclosing it – to turn the black heart into a loving heart and the darkness into light."

An extra service that should be performed after a release is completed and the person has been checked out clear, is to balance and energize the "chakras". The word "chakra" is a Sanskrit term meaning "wheel" and these energy centers are wheel-like vortices that are found along the spine on the surface of the etheric body. These centers are points of connection where energy flows from one of our four lower bodies to another. Although they are constantly rotating, they are often completely out of balance, at least one or more of them, and sometimes partially blocked. C. W. Leadbeater in his book The *Chakras,* [18] describes them thus:

"If we imagine ourselves to be looking straight down into the bell of a flower of the convolvulus type, we shall get some idea of the general appearance of a chakra. The stalk of the flower in each springs from a point in the spine... from which flowers shoot forth at intervals, showing the opening of their bells at the surface of the etheric body."

In the book, *I Will Arise* (book 1)[19] by Paola Hugh, the chakras are described as follows:

"'The chakras are like intricately and beautifully constructed valves; each one letting in just what it is attuned to in frequency of light, which light is a specific frequency or color. All chakras, when functioning harmoniously and unimpeded with congestive shadow, whirl at an incomprehensibly great speed, in a clockwise direction; and when whirling in the right direction, allow into the etheric vehicle only that substance of light or vital energy in concord with its function.

"Now when the magnetic field becomes clouded, congested with debris attracted into it by the magnetism of the mind impelled by destructive emotionism... the large arteries leading into the chakras become blocked or dammed... thus inhibiting the free flow of the necessary energy."

There are seven primary chakra centers, all known to the ancients: The root chakra is located over the pubic area at the base of the spine; the second or spleen chakra is below the navel and slightly to the left; the third chakra is over the solar plexus area; the fourth is over the heart center; the fifth is over the throat or thyroid center; the sixth over the center of the forehead just above the eyebrows, in Sanskrit called the Ajna center; and the seventh or crown chakra is over the top of the head. There is another chakra which we consider that is seldom mentioned (although there are many secondary chakras) and that is the mid-chest or Hermes center over the thymus gland.

These chakras are checked for balance and/or blockage and are healed and balanced with energy and the appropriate colors. It is important to know that these energy centers are the intermediary between you and the universe and it is very important that they be functioning properly.

As a rule, special exercises to open chakras or raise the "kundalini" (serpent fire at the base of the spine) should be avoided as it can be dangerous. These will open and unfold like the petals of a rose as we become balanced within ourselves, becoming more like the Christ or putting on the mind of Christ and learning to control every thought and feeling to the glory of God, as Anna Lee Skarin has brought out in her books.[20] The meditative practices we do should be for the purpose of achieving illumination, and the chakras will open and flower in due time.

However, there is a method of projecting color to the chakras which is totally harmless and helps to balance them. We do this for every patient after a release, but anyone can do it for himself. In our work, where we have only the person's picture or handwriting to use, we superimpose, by thought, the shape of a body with the corresponding chakras. Each one is named by number as we beam in the light with the left hand and the right hand holds the pendulum. Usually we get a counter-clockwise swing at first because the chakra is partially blocked. We beam in the violet light with the left hand until the pendulum slows down and gradually begins a clockwise swing. Then we beam in the appropriate color (by imaging it) until the swinging stops.

Some teachers have other opinions of what colors to use, but we prefer the colors of the spectrum. However, each chakra has its own combination of colors. If one does not feel sure of the right color, it is always safe to use the pure white Christ light which contains all colors, asking the intelligence of the chakra to take what it needs.

Now, begin with the first or root chakra. When counter-clockwise swinging stops, beam in a beautiful, clear rose-red from left hand. Continue until swinging stops.

The second chakra,below the navel, is balanced by a lovely orange glow. See your colors full of light!

The third chakra is at the solar plexus and we use a bright sunshine yellow. For the fourth or heart chakra, a joyous spring green is pictured.

Then we have the mid-chest or Hermes center. Most books do not consider this chakra so it is not numbered. But two very prominent spiritual teachers emphasize it – Dr. Brugh Joy and the late Inis Irene Hurd. The Hermes center is related to the Thymus gland and we use turquoise blue.

The fifth chakra is the throat center and nearly everyone needs work on this. Speaking negative, unkind words or misusing the voice can affect this chakra. We beam a beautiful blue, a little deeper than sky blue.

The sixth chakra is located between the eyebrows and slightly above and is often called the "Third Eye" center. We use a deep indigo blue, but full of light as through a stained glass window

Lastly, the seventh or Crown chakra at the top of the head. For this we use a glowing purple or violet shade. You may follow this with white.

When you have finished beaming this energy, harmonize all the chakras by a strong clockwise swing over them all. Then be sure to wash your hands, holding them under the faucet, over the wrists. This closes the circuit, neutralizing the energy.

When working with someone physically present, (in a prayerful, quiet state) hold the palm of the left hand over the root chakra at base of spine, but beam the light from the front, about fifteen inches out from the body. Beam violet from the left hand until swinging stops and goes clockwise. Then visualize the appropriate color from left hand and continue until swinging stops. Proceed with all chakras as above. When you have finished beaming this energy, be sure to wash your hands, as described above.

For those who may wish to have release work done for

themselves, friend or family, you may write to one of the names listed below. The work is done on a donation basis and the suggested offering is $30.00 per request. For Canada we suggest $35.00, and for other countries, $40.00. This is because postage rates are so high and we enclose extra material. Also be sure to include a photo or handwriting sample in ink.

A number of people have been trained and are very capably carrying on the work so please write to the name closest to your area or that you are drawn to. Bea Harper and Infinite Light have taken over most of Aloa's work by mail:

Bea Harper
P.O. Box 2021
Sedona, AZ 86339

INFINITE LIGHT
P.O. Box 31971
Tucson, AZ 85751

Joan & John Sheldon
P.O. Box 2381
Flagstaff, AZ 86004

Aloa Starr
P.O. Box 1396
Sedona, AZ 86339

FOOTNOTES

1. Omraam Mikhael Aivanhov, *Complete Works: Life, Vol.V* Prosveta USA,P.O.Box 49023, Los Angeles, CA.90049

2. Max Freedom Long, *The Secret Science At Work* (Los Angeles, CA Huna Research Publications, 1953)

3. Dr.George Hunt Williamson, *Other Tongues. Other Flesh* (Amherst, Wis. Amherst Press, 1953).

4. J.J. Hurtak *The Book of Knowledge: The Keys of Enoch* (Los Gatos, CA: The Academy for Future Science, P.O. Box FE, Los Gatos, CA 95030).

5. Denys Kelsy and Joan Grant, *Many Lifetimes* (New York: Pocket Books, 1968, 1 West 39th St., New York NY 10018) Out of Print.

6. Paola Hugh, *I Will Arise,* Two Vol. (Lakemont, GA:CSA Press, 30522 Vol.II. P,151

7. Peter Tompkins and Christopher Bird, *The Secret Life of Plants* New York, Harper & Row Publishers,Inc. 10022).

8. Morey Bernstein, *The Search for Bridey Murphy* (Garden City, New York: Doubleday & Company, 1959).

9. *Cosmic Awareness Communications* P.O. Box 115, Olympia, WA, 98507.

10. Paramahansa Yogananda, *Autobiography of a Yogi* (Los Angeles: Self Realization Fellowship, 1981).

11. Ellavivian Power *The Auric Mirror* (Alamogordo, NM: Ouimby Metaphysical Libraries, 88310)1973,Out of Print.

12. Levi,*The Aquarian Gospel of Jesus the Christ* (Marina del Rey, CA:DeVorss & Company, P.O.Box 550, 90294)1953

13. Taylor Caldwell, *The Glory and the Lightning* (New York:Fawcett Book Group, 201 E. 50th St. 10022) 1982, p.206

14. Calvin C. Girvin, *The Night Has a Thousand Saucers* (El Monte, CA: Understanding Publishing Co, 1015. Lexington) 1958.

15. I.L.Taimni, *The Science of Yoga* (Wheaton, IL: Theosophical Publishing House, 60187).

16. F. Scott Peck, M.D. *People of the Lie* (Simon & Schuster) 1983.

17. Carl A. Wicklund, M.D. *30 Years Among the Dead*(Van Nuys, CA: Newcastle Publishing Co. Inc. P.O. Box 7589, 91409) 1974

18. C. W. Leadbeater, *The Chakras* (Adyar Madras: The Theosophical Publishing House, India) 1958,p.3.

19. Paola Hugh, op.cit.p.70.

20. Anna Lee Skarin, *The Temple of God*(p.71); Man Triumphant p.252) DeVorss & Company, P.O.Box 550, Marina del Rey, CA 90294

BIBLIOGRAPHY

The author is grateful for permission to use excerpts from the works marked.*

Aivanhov, Omraam Mikhael. *LIFE, Complete Works*, Vol V. Prosveta, USA.

Askew, Stella. *How to Use a Pendulum*. Health Research, 1955.

Caldwell, Taylor. *Glory and the Lightning*. Doubleday and Company, 1974.

Fiore, Edith. *The Unquiet Dead*. A Dolphin Book, Doubleday and Company, Inc., 1987.

Hugh, Paola. *I Will Arise*. CSA Press, 1972.

Hall, Manly P. *Unseen Forces*. Philosophical Research Society, 1960.

Hurtak, J. J. *The Book of Knowledge: The Keys of Enoch*. The Academy for Future Science, 1977.

Krystal, Phyllis. *Cutting the Ties That Bind*. Element Books.

Leadbeater, C.W. *The Chakras*. The Theosophical Publishing House, 1958.

Levi. *Aquarian Gospel of Jesus Christ*. DeVorss & Company, 1953.

Long, Max Freedom. *Psychometric Analysis*. DeVorss & Company, 1953.

Long, Max Freedom. *The Secret Science at Work.*
Huna Research Publications, 1953.

Paramahansa Yogananda. **Autobiography of a Yogi.*
Self-Realization Fellowship, 1981.

Peck, F. Scott. *People of the Lie.*
Simon & Schuster, Inc, 1985.

Ryder, Daniel. *Breaking the Circle of Satanic Ritual Abuse.*
CompCare Publishers, 1992.

Wicklund, Carl A. *30 Years Among the Dead.*
Newcastle Publishing Company, Inc., 1974.

*Cosmic Awareness Communications.
For further information, write:
Box 115, Olympia, WA 98507

*Editions Prosveta, B.P.12.

INDEX